HORTUS

MISCELLANEOUS

A Gardener's Hodgepodge *of* Information **&** Instruction

LORENE EDWARDS FORKNER & LINDA PLATO

SASQUATCH BOOKS
SEATTLE

© 2007 by Lorene Edwards Forkner and Bruce Forestall

All rights reserved. No portion of this book may be reproduced or utilized in any form, or by any electronic, mechanical, or other means without the prior written permission of the publisher.

Printed in the United States of America
Published by Sasquatch Books

Distributed by Publishers Group West
15 14 13 12 11 10 09 08 07 06   9 8 7 6 5 4 3 2 1

Cover illustration/photograph: © 1995–2006 Missouri Botanical Garden
       http://www.illustratedgarden.org
Book design: Kate Basart/Union Pageworks
Interior illustrations: Kate Basart, Sarah Plein

Library of Congress Cataloging-in-Publication Data is available.

ISBN 1-57061-485-7

Sasquatch Books | 119 South Main Street, Suite 400 | Seattle, WA 98104
206.467.4300 | www.sasquatchbooks.com | custserv@sasquatchbooks.com

Preface

"The trouble with gardening is that it does not remain an avocation. It becomes an obsession."

PHYLLIS MCGINLEY (1905–1978), AMERICAN POET

Most gardening books and journals are made up of facts and material that to the mere mortal appear to embody the concept of arcane with a capital *A*. Lunar cycles, weather patterns, design principles that include not only three dimensions but also are further complicated by notions of time and space, color theory, taste tests, discipline, disease, pestilence, and physical labor—lots of physical labor, greed, envy, as well as most of the other deadly sins, and so much more—all held together by the thread of what many consider a dead language. Who cares?! We do.

Throughout history gardeners have recorded their discoveries, their tips, their successes, and their disappointments. This most ancient craft began as a physical necessity for survival, evolved to address domestic décor, and some would say has even been elevated to high art in the hands of the right creator. Hard science, mud-stained potting shed notes, old wives' tales, folklore and superstition, happenstance, and habit have all contributed to this body of knowledge that we gardeners find so compelling. We are assured by the discovery that nothing in the garden itself has really changed—the sun, a seed, some moisture, and you have begun. It is our culture and our selves that change in response to making a garden, and that is a process of endless fascination. Plant the world and grow yourself.

—LORENE EDWARDS FORKNER, JANUARY 2007

Acknowledgments

I'm lucky to have a number of everyday heroes in my life; people who inspire me, support me, make me laugh, and give me courage. All the same it is difficult to lose someone, however imperative you know that change to be. Disease, job relocation, and changing circumstances conspire to insert distance and great loss. It is at such times that I reach out to hold those near me with renewed esteem and wonder, as I also learn to recognize the gifts my heroes have left me. Linda Plato was a heroic woman with a keen sense of humor and a boundless creative energy. Thank you, Linda, for the gift of this book to write and thank you to Gary Luke and the staff at Sasquatch Books for their flying faith that I could do so. I have found it to be a uniquely wonderful creative exercise as someone more accustomed to crafting her work in the physical world of plants, soil, seasons, pests, and sore muscles.

Great thanks must go to Debra Prinzing, who throughout this process has been my constant ally, cheerleader, and confidant. Lois Pendleton and Susan Goetz carried Linda's work through to completion; their commitment and input kept Linda's voice in our final project. "It's all good."

Heartfelt thanks go to my staff at Fremont Gardens, who work so diligently in the service of the goddess flora. I am blessed to work among giants. I am grateful to my family, "the Tribe," and friends and neighbors who always root for my success.

My husband, James, and children, Hilary and Max, believe in me and forever shore me up through the hard parts. They make the journey fun and complete me.

—LORENE EDWARDS FORKNER

Count the Dots on Your Snowdrops

If a bee had three wings it would be a snowdrop ...

—COLETTE (1873–1954), FRENCH NOVELIST

Latin name: Galanthus (from the Greek *gala,* for milk, and *anthos,* for flower)

Common name: Snowdrop

Cultivation: There are approximately 209 *Galanthus* species, varieties, and named cultivars currently available in the United Kingdom. Snowdrops may be purchased as dormant bulbs in the fall or "in the green," that is, in active growth. Various species may bloom anywhere from late October through late March, with January and February offering peak "show."

Flower: All snowdrops produce a single flowering stem with a pendant white bell-shaped flower made up of 3 outer petals and 3 shorter inner petals lightly marked with green dots on their interior. (Double forms, of which there are many, have more petals.) The outer petals rise to a nearly horizontal position on warm days to attract early and active insects; the green markings on the inner petals guide pollinators to the center of the bloom.

Fragrance: Said to be that of a good honey.

What's the fuss?: Galanthophile—a serious collector of snowdrops. Galanthus Gala—a gathering of fellow collectors for the purpose of looking at the flowers. These events often feature lectures presented by fellow galanthophile experts, sales of specialty bulbs, and gardens where the lowly snowdrop doth shine.

Plays Well with Others

Mycorrhizal association: The relationship of a fungus with a higher plant, in which the fungus acts not as a parasite but as a partner, to both plants' mutual benefit.

Gin: A Gardener's Tipple

The preferred cocktail of many—esteemed plants-woman Rosemary Verey (1919–2001) included—gin is a careful distillation of grain spirits with heady botanicals that produce its unique aroma and flavor. Highly guarded proprietary recipes are kept secret but generally include some or all of the following: juniper, coriander, citrus peel, angelica, orrisroot, cardamom, cubeb berries (a pepper-like fruit), cassia bark, licorice, and cinnamon. It has been said that a good martini should taste like rain.

Horticultural Latin

A richly descriptive language of classification designed to inform, specify, and communicate across any language barrier throughout the world. While seemingly complex and intimidating to many, gardeners can take comfort in the fact that the International Code of Botanical Nomenclature (ICBN) is not a spoken language and therefore there are no hard and fast rules as to correct pronunciation, regardless of what snobbish plants people may imply. Hierarchical in nature, with every level of the entire plant kingdom neatly in its place, this language of plants can be a valuable tool in a gardeners' education.

Deconstructing the common maple tree, *Acer rubrum* 'Autumn Radiance':

- ☙ *The genus, or larger family of which this plant is a member, in this case* Acer, *is the first name and is always italicized with the first letter capitalized.*
- ☙ *This is followed by the species name, also italicized, which describes a specific trait of the plant; i.e.,* rubrum, *meaning scarlet. Subspecies (ssp.) or naturally occurring varieties (var.) refer to a further subset of traits and are also italicized.*
- ☙ *A unique cultivated variety or cultivar is indicated by a name in roman type within single quotation marks, as in 'Autumn Radiance'.*

Testing Seed Viability

1. Place 10 seeds on a damp paper towel sealed in a plastic bag.
2. Put plastic bag in a warm, bright location and watch for germination to occur.
3. Multiply the number of germinated seeds by 10 to gain a viability percentage: Greater that 70 percent, sow as directed; 40–60 percent, sow more heavily than indicated on seed package; less than 40 percent, replace seed with a fresh purchase.

Petal Plucking Rhyme

Market gardener, flower show-er,

Alpinist or orchid grower,

Bedder out, old plant collector,

Horticultural instructor,

Florist, botanist, Inorganic chemist,

"muck and mystery" man

Name Her

Abelia, Angelica, Aralia, Aster, Blossom, Camellia, Cecily, Cherry, Daisy, Fern, Flora, Ginger, Hazel, Heather, Holly, Iris, Ivy, Jasmine, Laurel, Leaf, Lilac, Lily, Magnolia, Meadow, Olivia, Orchid, Poppy, Posy, Primrose, Rose, Rosemary, Veronica, Violet

Name Him

Basil, Bay, Birch, Bud, Forrest, Linden, Moss, Oak, Reed, Rowan, Sage, Heath, Cliff

Name It

Cedar, Lake, Leaf, Rain, Sequoia

A Unique Spring Decoration

The cowslip, being a form of primrose, has a slender leafless stem bearing a terminal cluster of blossoms. To form a cowslip ball, break off the stems and join the heads of the flowers together with thread or string. Gather together tightly, with the stalk ends pointed to the inside and all blooms facing out. Cut the string short to pose the resulting ball atop a vase, or leave a length from which to suspend the ornament over your table. *Note:* Your cowslip ball will last longer if the flowers get a long soak right up to their heads before you begin.

Homegrown: A Recipe for Tobacco-Free Smoking

Mix 2 parts dried leaves of yellow coltsfoot to 1 part dried leaves of ground ivy. Said to cure some people of asthma and others of smoking.

Sweet Peas for Exhibition

Selected sweet peas for showing should have 4 or more flowers on a stem with the top flower still in bud.

1. Pick early on the day of the show, or if for a distant show, on the evening before.
2. Steep the flowers in cool water for no less than an hour.
3. Prepare bunches of a dozen or so of the selected flowers, and pack heads to tails on tissue in special boxes obtainable from the nursery.

Apple Bobbing

The best apple for bobbing is round, sweet, not too hard, and of medium size—not so small as to be gratuitous or so large as to bring disappointment. Red is the preferred color.

Suggested varieties: 'Braeburn', 'Empire', 'Gala', 'Jonathan', 'Macoun', 'Melrose', 'Pink Lady', 'Winesap'.

Early Native American Names for the Year's Full Moons

January	*Wolf moon*
February	*Snow moon*
March	*Worm moon*
April	*Pink moon**
May	*Corn-planting moon*
June	*Strawberry moon*
July	*Thunder moon*
August	*Red moon*
September	*Harvest moon*
October	*Hunters' moon*
November	*Beaver moon*
December	*Cold moon*

* *(referring to the dominant color of blooms during this month) or fish moon, sprouting grass moon, egg moon, and shad moon (clearly April has always been a busy month in the year)*

A Dainty Arrangement

A teacup makes a suitable container in which to show a dainty arrangement of blossoms. Also employable are the wine flute, juice glass, soup bowl, prescription vial, and the common milk bottle.

Scented Geraniums

Rose-scented: 'Atomic Snowflake', 'Attar of Roses', 'Candy Dancer', 'Charity', 'Crowfoot Rose', 'Dr. Livingstone' aka 'Skeleton Leaf Rose', 'Ice Crystal Rose', 'Lady Plymouth', 'Old Fashioned Rose', *Pelargonium capitatum*, 'Rober's Lemon Rose', 'Round Leaf Rose', 'Snowflake', 'Variegated Attar of Rose', 'Variegated Giant Rose'.

Mint-scented: 'Apple Mint', 'Joy Lucille', 'Mint Scented Rose', 'Peppermint', 'Peppermint Lace', 'Rollison's Unique'.

Lemon/citrus-scented: 'Citronella', 'Frensham', 'Galway Star', 'Ginger', 'Golden Lemon Crispum', 'Hansen's Wild Spice', 'Lemon', 'Lemon Balm', 'Lemon Fancy', 'Lemon Meringue', 'Lemonaire', 'Lime', 'Limoneum', 'Mabel Grey', 'Orange', 'Prince of Orange', 'Prince Rupert', 'Roger's Delight'.

Fruit- and nut-scented: 'Almond', 'Apple', 'Apricot', 'Coconut', 'Concolor Lace', 'Fringed Apple', 'Peach', 'Strawberry', 'Upright Coconut'.

Pungent-scented: 'Aroma', 'Brilliant', 'Brunswick', 'Chocolate Mint'.

How to Moss Pots

To blunt the rawness and effect the patina of age on new containers, paint a fresh terra-cotta pot with one or more of the following: yogurt or buttermilk containing live cultures, organic liquid plant food, or beer. Rub the pot with earth—that is, real soil, not sterile potting mix—and place in a continually damp, shady location for several weeks, giving the moss time to grow.

True Rosary Beads

Gather a large quantity of fragrant roses on a dry day and chop the petals very fine. Put the rose mash into an iron kettle on the stovetop and barely cover with distilled water. Bring up the temperature, but do not allow the mixture to boil; maintain for a period of 1 hour. Repeat this procedure for 3 days, adding more water if needed and being careful never to boil. During this time the rose paste will deepen to a rich black from its contact with the iron pot.

To form the beads, roll a pinch of the rose mixture into small balls with the palm of your hands. Pierce each resulting bead with a fine bamboo skewer and allow it to dry over a period of days. Gently rotate the beads each day as they dry to prevent them from adhering to the skewers. Once the beads are thoroughly dried, string them on a fine thread to form the rosary. When they are held by warm hands, a pleasing fragrance will rise and reputedly carry the petitioner's prayers to heaven.

A Simple Rose Vinegar

In a clean glass jar of high-quality white wine vinegar, place several handfuls of fresh-picked rose petals and leave to steep in a warm sunny spot for 24 hours. Strain the vinegar, decant into a decorative bottle, and store out of direct sunlight. A fresh linen handkerchief dipped in the rose vinegar and laid on the forehead is cooling and refreshing and is said to calm a headache.

A Gardener's Worst Fears

Alliumphobia	*Fear of garlic*
Anthophobia	*Fear of flowers*
Apiphobia	*Fear of bees*
Arachnophobia	*Fear of spiders*
Batonophobia	*Fear of plants*
Bufonophobia	*Fear of toads*
Dendrophobia	*Fear of trees*
Entomophobia	*Fear of insects*
Lachanophobia	*Fear of vegetables*
Melissophobia	*Fear of bees*
Mottephobia	*Fear of moths*
Myrmecophobia	*Fear of ants*
Ornithophobia	*Fear of birds*
Ranidaphobia	*Fear of frogs*
Rupophobia	*Fear of dirt*
Scoleciphobia	*Fear of worms*
Spheksophobia	*Fear of wasps*

Say It with Flowers

A Victorian parlor game in which decorous, some might say repressed, couples would send secret messages they could not bring themselves to utter by means of a bouquet of carefully chosen blossoms.

Allium	*Protection*
Amaryllis	*Pride*
Anemone	*Rejection*
Aster	*Loyalty*
Bachelor's button	*Solitude*
Buttercup	*Childishness*
Carnation	*Faithfulness*
Crocus	*Youthful glee*
Dahlia	*Instability*
Daisy	*Purity*
Dogwood	*Patience*
Forget-me-not	*Fond memory*
Freesia	*Tranquility*
Gardenia	*Hospitality and grace*
Heather (red)	*Passion*
Heather (white)	*Protection from the consequences of passion*
Heliotrope	*Devotion*
Hollyhock	*Fertility*
Honeysuckle	*Bonds of love*
Hyacinth	*Young love*
Hydrangea	*Cheek*
Jasmine	*Good fortune*
Lavender	*Distrust*

Lilac	*Melancholy*
Lily	*Innocence*
Magnolia	*Poise*
Marigold	*Bittersweet*
Narcissus	*Vainglory*
Nasturtium	*Prank*
Orchid	*Rapture*
Pansy	*Thoughtfulness*
Peony	*Prudence*
Poppy	*Dreams*
Primrose	*Hope*
Queen Anne's lace	*Self-reliance*
Quince	*Temptation*
Red rose	*Love*
Rosemary	*Remembrance*
Snapdragon	*Revenge*
Sunflower	*Power*
Sweet pea	*Lasting pleasure*
Tulip	*Declaration of love*
Violet	*Modesty*
White rose	*Silence*
Wisteria	*Obedience*
Yellow rose	*Jealousy*
Zinnia	*Absence*

Beware the Pogonip

"Pogonip" is a meteorological term that describes an uncommon occurrence—frozen fog.

Safe Ice Thickness

Ice Thickness	Permissible Load
3 inches	Single person on foot
4 inches	Group in single file
7½ inches	Passenger car (2 ton gross)
8 inches	Light truck (2½ ton gross)
10 inches	Medium truck (3½ ton gross)
12 inches	Heavy truck (8 ton gross)
15 inches	10 tons
20 inches	25 tons
30 inches	70 tons
36 inches	110 tons

Note: Measures are for solid, clear, blue/black pond and lake ice. Slush ice has only half the strength of blue ice. The strength of river ice is 15 percent less than blue ice.

To Gauge Wind Speed

10 mph . . . . . *You can feel the wind on your face.*
20 mph . . . . . *Small branches move and dust or snow is raised.*
30 mph . . . . . *Large branches move and the wind whistles.*
40 mph . . . . . *Whole trees bend.*

Steal a March on Spring

Forcing branches for winter color and fragrance:

1. Prune branches at least 12 inches long using clean, sharp pruners so as not to bruise the wood and leave the wound open to weakness and disease. Immediately plunge the cut branches into a bucket of warm water and bring indoors.
2. Completely immerse the cut branches in a large tub of water for 8–12 hours to encourage the plant to break dormancy.
3. Place branches in a vase or bucket of water and put in a room with good light away from any heat source. Mist occasionally to maintain a humid environment and watch for the buds to swell until they burst into a precocious spring bloom.

Suggested plants for forcing: Apple, birch, buttercup winter hazel, cherry, dogwood, elderberry, forsythia, lilac, magnolia, maple, pear, quince, redbud, spirea, willow, witch hazel.

Various Beans

❧

adzuki, 'Anasazi', 'Appaloosa', 'Baccicia', 'Bayou', 'Black Appaloosa', 'Black Calypso', 'Black Nightfall', 'Black-seeded Runner', black turtle, 'Black Valentine', bolita, borlotti, buckskin, 'Butterscotch Calypso', California cranberry, cannellini, 'Cave', chestnut lima, 'Christmas lima', 'Coach', cranberry, 'Dalmatian', eastern cannellini, 'European Soldier', 'Eye of Goat', fava, 'Flor de Junio', French horticultural, French navy, 'Garboncito', 'Gigante', 'Good Mother Stallard', green flageolet, 'Jackson Wonder', 'Jacob's Cattle', 'Madeira', marrow, 'Mexican Red', 'Molasses Face', 'Mortgage Lifter', 'Orca', 'Painted Pony', pebble, 'Peruano', 'Pinquito', 'Purple Appaloosa', 'Raquel', rattlesnake, 'Red Appaloosa', 'Red Calypso', red flageolet, 'Red Nightfall', 'Repokeb', rice, 'Rio Zappe', runner cannellini, 'Scarlet Runner', 'Snowcap', southern checker pea, specialty black garbanzo, 'Speckled Brown Cow', split baby garbanzo, 'Steuben Yellow Eye', Swedish brown, 'Sweet White', 'Taylor's Horticultural', 'Tiger Eye', 'Tocomares Chocolate', 'Tongues of Fire', 'Trout', 'Vallarta', 'Vermont Cranberry', 'Wild Rice', 'Wren's Egg', 'Yaqui Ojo de Cabra', 'Yellow Eye', yellow flageolet, 'Yellow Indian Woman', 'Yin Yang'

Temperature Conversions

Celsius		Fahrenheit
0	*Freezing point of water*	32
10	*A warm winter day*	50
20	*A mild spring day*	68
30	*Almost hot*	86
37	*Normal body temperature*	98.6
40	*Heat wave conditions*	104
100	*Boiling point of water*	212

Birthstones and Flowers

January	Garnet	Snowdrop
February	Amethyst	Primrose
March	Aquamarine	Violet
April	Diamond	Daisy
May	Emerald	Hawthorn
June	Pearl	Rose
July	Ruby	Water lily
August	Peridot	Poppy
September	Sapphire	Morning glory
October	Opal	Hops
November	Topaz	Chrysanthemum
December	Turquoise	Holly

Garden Stain Removal

Grass, flowers, and foliage: Work soap or detergent into the stained article, then rinse in cool water. If fabric is colorfast, sponge the stain with alcohol. Persistent stains may be treated with a chlorine or peroxide bleach.

Mud: Let stain dry, then brush well to remove soil. If stain remains, treat as for grass, flowers, and foliage. Stains from iron-rich clays not removed by this method should be treated as rust stains.

Rust: (1) Cream of tartar method: Boil the stained article in a solution of 4 teaspoons' cream of tartar per pint of water. Boil until stain is removed. Rinse thoroughly. (2) Lemon juice method: Spread the stained portion over a pan of boiling water and squeeze lemon juice on it. Alternately, sprinkle table salt on the stain, squeeze lemon juice on it, and spread the fabric in the sun to dry. Rinse thoroughly and repeat if necessary.

Berries: Remove excess berry with a spoon or dull knife. Thoroughly saturate the stain with cold water and work soap or liquid detergent into the area. Allow to stand for 5 minutes. With stained article stretched over a bowl in the sink, pour hot water through the back of the stain to force it out of the fabric. Early treatment will grant the best results.

Leaves of Three, Let Them Be

Poison ivy, poison oak, and poison sumac—typically identified by their clusters of 3 shiny leaflets—are the major contact poison plants found in North America. Signs and symptoms of contact include itching skin and blisters, which are the effects of a harsh resin found in the leaves. Some relief may be had by diluting and washing away the resin with a strong laundry soap and water followed by the application of wet dressings. Take care to not rupture the blisters. Oatmeal baths may help to relieve any itching. More serious consequences can result from chewing the leaves of poison ivy or inhaling the smoke of plants being burned, both of which will cause painful swelling in the throat, accompanied by fever and weakness. Professional medical treatment should be sought at once.

Dog Days

Named for the Dog Star, Sirius, which is dominant in the summer sky, these generally hot and lazy days of the year were traditionally thought to last from July 3 through August 11.

Dancing Bees

Upon returning to the hive, a scout bee will communicate the location of a food source—too distant to be seen or smelled—by means of a dance. Other bees gather around and imitate her movements, taking note of the scent on her of the various flowers she has visited. The dancing worker bee will differentiate her moves to tell the rest of the hive whether the food source is relatively near (circular dance) or a greater distance away (figure-eight dance).

Common Garden Injuries

Roughly one in every five DIY injuries occurs during gardening activities:

- *Sunburn*
- *Heat exhaustion*
- *Lawn-mower injuries, which typically include open wounds, eye injuries, and bone fractures of the hands and feet*
- *Repetitive-stress injuries, most often of the wrist and upper body*
- *Back strain*
- *Dehydration*
- *Insect bite/reaction*
- *Contact dermatitis*

lab·y·rinth: A garden feature consisting of a pattern of rhythmic winding paths having one way in and one way out of the pattern, with no choices to be made along its passage by the walker. Walking the labyrinth is said to inspire a meditative and calming mindset representing one's journey through life.

maze: A garden feature generally constructed of tall hedges composed of evergreen plants, designed with humor and the intention of causing a person walking its winding, circuitous paths to lose their way. *Note:* Should you ever find yourself lost in a maze, place your hand on either the right or left wall and follow its every turning. You cannot fail to emerge.

Gardeners on the Go
Another Horticultural (?) Roadside Attraction

One type of gardener is loathe to leave their garden for any reason, for fear they might miss something of import—a flower's precious bloom, an overlooked insect poised to despoil. Or, simply overcome by that day's weeding and watering chores, they haven't the energy for anything else. They are, in essence, every bit as bound to the site as the roots of the plants they tend. However, most gardeners are among the most inquisitive and observant of all travelers, constantly and tirelessly searching out gardens and interesting environments near and far. Countless guidebooks are penned and tours organized that cater to traveling gardeners, with listings of public and formal gardens in every corner of the land. For the horticulturally curious traveler with an appreciation for the eccentric, the open road is rich with slightly offbeat landscapes.

Gardeners on the Go with a Spiritual Bent

Consider the following slightly offbeat landscapes when choosing your next garden getaway destination.

Cullman, AL: The Ave Maria Grotto. A miniature artificial cave is the central feature of a collection of 125 artfully crafted, miniature replicas of some of the world's most holy sites, shrines, and buildings created by Brother Joseph Soettl, a Benedictine monk of Saint Bernard Abbey, all set within a beautifully landscaped 4-acre park.

Pittsburgh, PA: Rodef Shalom Biblical Botanical Garden. Another Holy Land replica featuring biblical plants and plants with biblical names. Each year a special display, staffed and maintained entirely by volunteers, is created around a featured topic with attendant educational programs, lectures, and publications. Past features:

1. 1989 Drugs and Pharmaceuticals in the Early Biblical World
2. 1993 Fragrance through the Ages—Perfume, Incense, and Cosmetics
3. 1997 Papyrus to Paper
4. 2001 Botanical Symbolism in World Religions

Lucedale, MS: Palestine Gardens. A 5-acre scale model of the Holy Land at the time of Jesus, complete with the river Jordan, the Dead Sea, Bethlehem, and Jerusalem.

New Harmony, IN: The Labyrinth. A complicated series of winding paths and obstacles created in the early nineteenth century by Harmonists—a group of German immigrants who settled in Indiana to await the return of Christ—as a form of active meditation and to illustrate the difficult journey of life.

Colebrook, NH: Shrine of Our Lady of Grace. Formally recognized by the Roman Catholic Church this beautiful 25-acre setting contains more than fifty intricately carved granite and marble devotional monuments and is home to the ritual Blessing of the Motorcycles held each year since 1976 at the beginning of the summer riding season. A sort of sacramental Sturgis.

Ommmmm

The practice of burning herbs in a ceremonial way, called "smudging," is common among many traditions. It is thought that the resulting smoke not only releases the herb's fragrance, but also its unique energies.

California bay . . . .*Healing protection*
Cedar, cypress, juniper . . . . .*Consecration*
Desert sage. . . . .*Clearing negativity*
Fennel . . . .*Repelling evil energy*
Fir, hemlock, pine, spruce. . .*Purifying and cleansing*
Kinnikinnick . . . .*Calming*

Mexican tea . . . .*Establishing healthy boundaries*
Mint. . . . .*Uplifting*
Mugwort . . . .*Divination*
Mullein . . . .*Calming*
Saint's herb . . . .*Promoting courage*
Sweet grass . . . .*Protection*

Weather Portents

❧ *Red sky at morn, sailors be warned.*

❧ *Three foggy mornings in a row signifies rain.*

❧ *A halo around the moon is a sign that rain is on its way; the bigger the halo, the sooner the shower.*

❧ *Red sky at night, sailors' delight.*

❧ *If the rising full moon is clear, expect pleasant weather.*

❧ *Morning glories, dandelions, daisies, wood sorrel, and pimpernel close their blossoms before it rains, while sunflowers raise their heads in anticipation.*

❧ *Flowers will be more fragrant just before a rainfall.*

❧ *When you can step on three daisies in the lawn, spring has arrived.*

❧ *A mild January will bring a chilly May.*

❧ *The same amount of rain that falls in March will also fall in June.*

❧ *Never trust the sky in the month of July.*

❧ *A warm October indicates a cold February.*

The Seven Principles of Xeriscape Gardening

Xeri·scaping: Landscaping for water management and conservation (*xeri* means dry in Greek).

1. Appropriate plant choice and placement: Do not attempt an English-style cottage garden in Arizona.
2. Add organic material to the existing garden soil to maximize water retention and good tilth.
3. Lose the lawn: While a broad green sward is a common ideal, it is an unrealistic goal where water is at a premium, to wit, golf greens in Vegas?
4. Plant zones: Group plants with similar cultural requirements together to make the best use of water resources. Wet with wet; dry with dry.
5. Mulch to keep soil temperatures cool and to help retain water in the plants' root zones.
6. Only water the landscape when and where needed.
7. Appropriate maintenance of plants, soil conditions, and irrigation tools is critical to the success of the above principles.

Heaven on Earth

100 blue flowers for the garden (A = annual, B = bulb, P = perennial, S = shrub, V = vine): 'Miss Jekyll' love-in-a-mist (A), forget-me-not (P), lily of the Nile (P), bellflower (P), glory-of-the-snow (B), *Allium caeruleum* (B), blue windflower (B), grape hyacinth (B), bluebeard shrub (S), lungwort (P), Siberian forget-me-not (P), 'Georgia Blue' veronica (P), amsonia (P), leadwort (P), bog sage (P), 'China Blue' fumitory (P), wisteria (V), bluebells (B), camassia (B), false indigo (P), meadow cranesbill (P), shrubby teucrium (P), nemesia (A), cupid's-dart (P), Dutch iris (B), Siberian iris (P), blue lobelia (P), Russian sage (P), cornflower (P), bachelor's button (A), 'Butterfly Blue' scabiosa (P), catmint (P), butterfly bush (S), Jacob's ladder (P), 'Cambridge Blue' lobelia (A), 'Hewitt's Double' meadow rue (P), society garlic (B), 'True Blue' penstemon (P), spiderwort (P), Parma violet (P), 'The Governor' lupine (P), pimpernel (P), Italian alkanet (P), 'Blue Barlow' columbine (P), borage (A), globe thistle (P), grass pea (A, V), baby blue-eyes (A), honeywort (A), garden squill (B), spring vetch (P), periwinkle (P), 'President Grevey' lilac (S), mealycup sage (A), dayflower (P), gentian sage (P), monkshood (P), delphinium (P), 'Nikko Blue' hydrangea (S), gentian (P), 'Heavenly Blue' morning glory (A, V), sea holly (P), Himalayan blue poppy (P), 'Monch' aster (P), California lilac (S), potato vine (V), 'May Night' salvia (P), butterfly pea (A, V), Texas blue bonnet (A), plumbago (V), balloon flower (P), 'Blue Bird' rose of Sharon (S), 'Sky Blue' nolana (A), wild chicory (P), larkspur (A), viper's bugloss (P), Canterbury bells (P), browallia (A), blue hyssop (P), globe gilia (A), blue-eyed grass (P), phacelia (A), Virginian bluebells (P), shoo-fly plant (A), ageratum (A), flax (P), blue star creeper (P), 'Grace Ward' lithodora (P), 'Hidcote Blue' lavender (S), 'Perl d'Azur' clematis (V), bugle (P), blue oat grass (P), comfrey (P), pasqueflower (P), blue hyacinth bean (A, V), shooting star (B), heliotrope (P), 'Jackman's Blue' rue (P), Chinese plumbago (P), blue fescue (P).

Panel
Closed board
Slatted or lath
Picket
Post and rail
Single rail
Post and rope or chain
Paling
Riggle/wriggle
Bamboo
Wattle
Hairpin wire
Chain link
Wrought or cast iron

fedge: A hybrid between a fence and a hedge. A vigorous climber of sorts is trained to smother a vertical framework of timber and wire. The appearance is that of a hedge, but it is much quicker to establish.

hor·ti·cul·tur·al sport: An atypical plant form or mutation that has arisen spontaneously.

Fenway's Ivy

Peter del Tredici, director of Harvard University's Arnold Arboretum, discovered an unusual sport of Boston ivy in 1988 growing on the walls of Fenway Park, home field to baseball's Boston Red Sox. That (horticultural) sport is now bred and distributed as *Parthenocissus tricuspidata* 'Fenway Park'. Common Boston ivy is a rapacious climbing vine capable of reaching 60 feet that adheres to any surface by means of its tendrils. The foliage is typically a deep green throughout spring and summer, turning a rich brilliant red in the fall before dropping its leaves. 'Fenway Park' is distinguished by its new golden foliage that remains yellow when the plant is grown in full sun.

Choices for the Garden's Ground Plane

brick, crushed stone, timber decking, gravel, cobbles, exposed aggregate, asphalt, precast cement slabs, concrete blocks, tumbled or cut natural stone, pebble mosaic, woodchips, granite setts, slate, marble slabs, synthetic lumber, sawn log cross-sections, bark chips, terra-cotta tile, poured concrete, raked sand, turf, moss, low-growing groundcovers

Brick Patterns

Stack bond

Running bond

Herringbone

Diagonal herringbone

Basket weave

Half basket weave

Jack on Jack

Flemish bond

English bond

Colonial bond

Pinwheel

Paradise

For the devout Muslim, Islamic gardens represent a terrestrial
paradise, an Earthly taste of heaven to come.

Control Issues

Pollard: A woodland management technique traditionally employed
to produce crops of firewood or lumber in which trees on a single
stem are cut back to a height just above that of grazing livestock.

Coppice: A technique similar to pollarding in which trees and
shrubs are cut back all the way to ground level. Today this
method is more generally used to enhance the ornamental value
of plants with attractive juvenile growth.

Pleach: A technique in which tree branches are trained in a single
horizontal plane above a clear stem, eventually knitting together
with the branches of adjacent trees forming an elevated hedge, as
it were.

Hedge: A series of shrubs or trees planted in a line and trimmed
to maintain a uniform height and width.

Topiary: The traditional craft of training and pruning plants into
a variety of forms, be they strongly geometric or whimsically
representational.

Cordon: A restrictive form of pruning traditionally employed
on fruit trees to maximize production in a limited space. The

cordon, a single stem along which multiple short fruiting spurs are encouraged, can be trained vertically, at an angle, or as two or more parallel arms.

Espalier: A restrictive form of pruning consisting of a central stem supporting several tiers of paired horizontal branches on which short fruiting spurs are maintained. Espaliered fruit trees are often trained against a southern wall, where they benefit from retained heat, thus ripening their crop more quickly.

Parterres and knots: Meticulously clipped plants that form intricate geometric patterns representing the gardener's ultimate control over the garden; generally designed to be viewed from above for the most impressive display.

Garden Structures

Arch: A rounded structure of wood or metal upon which vines may be grown; often placed at an entrance or to span a path.

Pergola: A continuous series of arches placed at intervals along a path.

Tunnel: A series of connected arches placed more closely in sequence, often clothed in vines to create a sense of enclosure; an effective device for linking one part of the garden to another, as there must be a specific destination.

Arbor: An overhead structure enclosed on one side to provide shelter for a bench or table and chairs; oftentimes used as a focal point within a garden.

Awning: A device made from fabric on a generally retractable frame placed to cast shade and provide pleasant seating areas within the garden or to shield windows from direct sun.

Conditioning Cut Flowers

Tools

Sharp knife, scissors, or clippers
Bleach or flower food
Cool clean water
Plastic or nonmetal buckets for soaking
Vases and containers for arranging
Hammer, rose thorn stripper (optional)

Method

1. Fill a clean bucket with cool water, adding 1 tablespoon of flower food or 1 teaspoon of bleach to every gallon of water to prevent bacterial growth (which will shorten a flower's vase life).

2. Working with the cut flowers, remove all foliage that might fall below the water line as well as any damaged or excess foliage and all thorns.

3. Cut at least 2 inches off the bottom of each stem at a sharp angle to maximize surface area for water uptake. Plunge cut stems immediately into prepared water and allow to rest and soak for an hour or two before final arranging.

4. Split or mash woody plants with a hammer at least 2 inches above the cut to further encourage these tougher stems to absorb water. Most woody stems will benefit from a warm-water soak for their first hour following a fresh cut.

5. Arrange conditioned and well-hydrated flowers in a clean vase or container and maintain proper water levels at all times. Protect arrangements from temperature extremes, dry air, and drafts. Light and warmth encourage development in cut flowers, while cool darkness slows the process down. Use these factors to prolong vase life or hurry buds along toward blooming.

Special Techniques

- *Stems and branches that ooze a milky sap* must have all cuts sealed to prevent bleeding. Dip cut ends in boiling water for 10–15 seconds or hold over an open flame to seal cuts; protect flowers from direct exposure to the heat source. Apply to poppies, all euphorbias, acanthus, hollyhocks, clematis, hellebores, and hydrangeas.

- *To revive wilted flowers,* recut stems and completely immerse in a bath of tepid water—blooms, leaves, stems, and all. Camellias, peonies, roses, lilies, some orchids, violets, and many other flowers benefit from this treatment. But avoid this technique with especially delicate flowers and those blooms with fuzzy foliage.

- *To straighten curled stems,* most notably tulips, carefully wrap the entire bunch of flowers in damp newspaper to form a straight tube, secure with a rubber band, and submerge in water for an hour or two.

al·lée: A planted avenue of paired trees with strongly vertical growth habits; often sited at the entry of an estate to impress approaching visitors.

One for You, Twenty for Me

Self-seeding perennials:

Columbine (*Aquilegia vulgaris*)
Dame's rocket (*Hesperis matronalis*)
Drumstick allium (*Allium sphaerocephalum*)
Forget-me-not (*Myosotis sylvestris*)
Foxglove (*Digitalis purpurea*)
Garden stock (*Matthiola incana*)
Golden Bowles' grass (*Milium effuseum* 'Aureum')
Golden feverfew (*Tanacetum parthenium* 'Aureum')
Golden fumitory (*Corydalis lutea*)
Hardy cyclamen (*Cyclamen hederifolium*)
Lady's-mantle (*Alchemilla mollis*)
Miss Wilmott's ghost (*Eryngium gigateum*)
Money plant (*Lunaria rediviva*)
Oriental hellebore (*Helleborus* ×*hybridus*)
Peruvian verbena (*Verbena bonariensis*)
Rose campion (*Lychnis coronaria*)
Welsh poppy (*Meconopsis cambrica*)
Windflower (*Anemone blanda*)

Care and Cultivation of the Common Carrot

Carrots perform best in deep, light, rich soils. Avoid overenriching the soil to prevent rank growth. Take care to remove all stones, clods, and anything else that will cause the carrots to stunt or fork. For this reason, raised beds are especially effective in producing well-developed, straight roots.

The tiny seeds may be sown as soon as the soil can be worked. Because carrots are slow to germinate, mixing the seed with more quickly sprouting lettuces or radishes will help to define the seeding area. It is better to sow the seed sparsely than to rely too much on thinning for eventual proper spacing, as the scent of the thinnings being removed will attract the carrot rust fly whose larvae will quickly destroy the crop by tunneling through the roots and spoiling them for the table.

Weeds: Some of Nature's Most Prolific Opportunists

Poetically described as a plant whose features are not yet recognized or any plant in the wrong place, in fact weeds are a group of plants that have developed amazing reproductive capabilities and tough constitutions that allow them to survive where other more "civilized" plants cannot. In this way weeds play a valuable environmental role in covering bare ground and preventing devastating soil erosion.

Keeping the ground covered, whether with mulch, groundcovers, or spreading plants, is the best defense against weeds gaining a foothold in the garden. If they do—and they will, being weeds and gardeners being mere mortals—take care to remove any seed heads as they form before they have the opportunity to spread their prolific progeny to any other available scrap of bare earth.

Make Weeds Work for You

The following weeds are *not* recommended for planting in the garden. These are merely suggestions for making good use of that which we cannot get rid of. A knowledgeable gardener might put these weeds' unique properties to good use in the garden.

Mustard: This family (alyssum, phlox, kale, etc.) will clean up salty soils and can be planted where they will improve roadside beds following winter de-icing, and they will perform well in areas where soils are high in naturally occurring salts.

Geranium: Many types of this large family of plants have proved fatal or at least toxic to Japanese beetles, a pernicious pest found east of the Rocky Mountains that can wreak havoc with garden ornamentals.

Horsetail: An especially persistent weed in wet soils, horsetail is an effective antifungal agent when brewed into a strong tea, cooled, and sprayed on plants subject to mildews and fungus.

Stinging nettles: High in potassium and calcium and extremely nutritious for both garden and gardener alike. Apply to soils as a tea or add plants to the compost pile. To protect oneself from the nasty sting of fresh nettles caused by the fine hairs along their stem and leaves, wear protective clothing when harvesting.

Comfrey: Also high in potassium and a valuable addition to the compost. Treat a bruise with a comfrey poultice.

Bringing the Outdoors In
Paint Choices for Interior Decoration

Alfalfa, Arboretum, Aspen Leaf, Crown of Laurel, Forest, Fresh Lime, Fresh Melon, Herb Garden, Hot Pepper, Irish Ivy, June Bud, Lime Twist, Pale Wintergreen, Pastel Sage, Quiet Knoll, Rolling Meadow, Sassafras Tea, Shamrock, Shy Blossom, Southern Pine, Spearmint, Spirea, Spring Fest, Spring Fling, Summer Rain, Summer Savory, Sweet Leaf, Tree House, Topiary, Victorian Sage, Window Garden, Zesty Lime

BIG FOOD

'2444 Oxheart' carrot	6-inch by 4-inch roots weighing up to 1 pound
Armenian yard-long cucumber	2- to 3-foot-long fruit
'Canoe Creek Colossal' melon	8 to 15 pounds average fruit
'Colossal Long Red' mangel beet	Roots to 2 feet weighing up to 15 pounds

'Cow Horn' okra	10- to 12-inch-long slender pods on 6- to 7-foot-tall plants
'Dill's Atlantic Giant' pumpkin	Fruit to 500 pounds not uncommon
'Giant Aconcagua' pepper	11-inch by 2½-inch frying peppers
'Giant Argonaut' winter squash	30-pound fruit
'Giant Cobb Gem' watermelon	125-pound fruit
'Old German' tomato	2-pound red-striped golden fruit
'Southern American Flakkee' carrot	8- to 9-inch roots being 2 inches at the shoulder
'Saint Valery' carrot	Roots 10 to 12 inches by 2 to 3 inches
'Tropic Giant' cabbage	Mature heads 12 inches in diameter weighing up to 15 pounds
Yard-long asparagus bean	2- to 3-foot-long beans

Bernard Lavery of the United Kingdom grew the world's largest cabbage in 1989. Said cabbage was grown outside in his garden in Wales receiving no special treatment other than a high-nitrogen liquid feed applied directly to the root region twice a week. Harvesting the monster vegetable was a complicated affair. Ironically the award winner, weighing in at a whopping 124 pounds, was Lavery's second choice. His prime specimen, reputed to have been one-third larger than the record breaker, broke into pieces during harvest. Digging methods were altered and the second cabbage was dug and transported 210 miles to the Worldwide Giant Vegetable Championship being held in Alton Towers. While Lavery was quite pleased with his award, he still thinks about "the one that got away," estimated to have been at least 150 pounds.

Congratulations . . . It's a Cabbage?!

Naturally small when mature, picked young or sown at close density for cut-and-come-again production, these vegetables are all suitable for container gardening and are appropriate choices for gardeners with limited space:

'Pronto' beet
Baby head cabbage
'Baby Babette' carrots
'Parmex' carrot
Baby corn
Thai green pea eggplant
'Tom Thumb' lettuce
'Sugar Baby' melon
Micro greens
Baby pearl onions
'Baby bell' pepper
'Jingle Bell' pepper
'Baby Boo' pumpkin
'Easter Egg' radish
'Sweet Dumpling' winter squash
'Spoon' tomatoes
'Bambino F1 Mini-Courgette' zucchini

Important Questions to Consider
Before Planning Your Garden

Complete the following checklist in a thoughtful manner—
either on your own or with the help of a designer—to create a
garden space that is uniquely suited to your site, your conditions,
and your preferences.

Do you intend to actually spend time in the garden? When?

☐ Days
☐ Evenings after work
☐ Weekends at the summer place

Do you prefer open, exposed space or enclosed, sheltered areas?

☐ Favorite childhood hangout: Tree house or cave?
☐ Preferred vacation destination: Beach or deep woods?

*What existing degrees of sun, shade, and in-between are you dealing
with? Are there changes to consider in order to achieve the character of the
space you identified previously?*

☐ Call the arborist
☐ Call the builder

*City brownstone or suburban ranch? Consider repeating elements of your
home's architecture in the garden to tie the two together.*

☐ Mellow brick
☐ Poured concrete
☐ Urban grit
☐ Bucolic reverie

Make note of significant sightlines from inside the house out to the garden.

- ☐ Fabulous view
- ☐ Nosy neighbors

How do you move through the space to get to entrances, the driveway or garage, and any utility spaces?

- ☐ Welcoming entry
- ☐ Dominating driveway
- ☐ Oh yeah, utility space

Where do you live?

- ☐ Hot summers
- ☐ Extreme winters
- ☐ Harsh wind
- ☐ Clammy humidity
- ☐ Constant rain

How much time are you willing to allot to the creation and maintenance of your garden?

- ☐ 1 hour a week
- ☐ 10 hours a week
- ☐ Daylight hours of the week

Who will do the work?

- ☐ Homeowner
- ☐ Staff

What is your budget?

- ☐ Budget?
- ☐ $
- ☐ $$$

Nighttime Scented/Blooming Plants

Pollinated by moths and other nocturnal creatures attracted to
their heavy scents and aided by the way white flowers shine in
the moonlight, these plants emit their fragrances after sunset:

Cereus cactus
Datura
Evening primrose
Evening-scented stock
Flowering tobacco
Honeysuckle
Moonflower
Night-scented phlox

Horticultural Heartthrobs

love-lies-bleeding, love-in-a-mist, kiss-me-over-the-garden-gate,
cupid's-dart, bleeding heart, bridal wreath spirea, passionflower,
exotic love, love in a puff, hearts-a-burstin', purple love grass,
lovage, forget-me-not, painted lady runner bean, heartleaf
bergenia, bachelor's button

USDA Plant Hardiness Zones

The hardiness zone system developed by the U.S. Department of Agriculture and updated regularly is based on the average annual minimum temperature for each zone.

	Farenheit	Celsius
Zone 1	below −50	below −46
Zone 2	−50 to −40	−46 to −40
Zone 3	−40 to −30	−40 to −34
Zone 4	−30 to −20	−34 to −29
Zone 5	−20 to −10	−29 to −23
Zone 6	−10 to 10	−23 to −18
Zone 7	10 to 20	−18 to −12
Zone 8	20 to 30	−12 to 1.7
Zone 9	30 to 40	1.7 to 1.1
Zone 10	30 to 40	1.1 to 4
Zone 11	above 40	above 4

Contra Vim Mortis/Crescit Salvia In Hortis

The above couplet, which roughly translates as "against power of death/sage grows in the garden," only hints at the many and varied uses of garden herbs throughout history. Whether considering their medicinal relevance, utilitarian application in the dye and fragrance industries, their savory presence at the table, or their ornamental use in gardens both cottage and formal, herbs must be regarded as highly useful and a valuable component of a well-lived life.

How to Brew a Good Cup of Herbal Tea

True "tea" is an infusion of the leaves of *Camellia sinensis*, so herbal teas are more accurately called "tisanes."

1. In a warmed teapot, place 2–3 tablespoons coarsely chopped fresh or 1–2 tablespoons dried herbs or a mixture of herbs. Cover with a teacup's worth of freshly boiled water for each finished serving.
2. Steep for several minutes or until desired strength is achieved. Strength must be determined by flavor, not color, as many infusions will remain a light green or straw color.
3. Strain into a cup and serve with honey or lemon if desired. For a refreshing noncaffeinated iced tea, chill finished tisane and serve over ice.

A Digestive Tea

2 parts peppermint
1 part tarragon
1 part lemon balm
1 part chamomile flowers
1 part anise or fennel seed
½ part rosemary

Prepare as for herbal tea, above. Inhale the fragrance and sip slowly following a heavy meal to aid digestion.

A Soothing Floral Tea

2 parts chamomile flowers
1 part lemon balm
1 part catnip
1 part lavender flowers
1 part peppermint
1 part rose petals
1 part lemongrass (optional)
A pinch of nutmeg to taste

Prepare as for herbal tea, above. Find a comfortable chair and sip tea slowly to let go of stress and promote relaxation.

An Uplifting Tea

3 parts lemon balm
1 part lavender flowers
1 part rose petals
1 part spearmint
1 part Saint-John's-wort
1 part marjoram

Prepare as for herbal tea. Drink up to 3 cups a day to promote feelings of well-being.

A Women's Tonic

6 parts raspberry leaves
4 parts chamomile flowers
2 parts rose petals
1 part ground licorice root
1 part rosemary
Fresh ginger root

Prepare as for herbal tea, placing a ¼-inch slice of fresh ginger in each teacup served. Drink hot or chilled, but no more than 1 cup daily.

Turf Blends

Proper site evaluation and the choice of an appropriate blend of grass seed will make the difference between a thick sward of green and a struggling threadbare patch. Most turf mixes also contain a "nurse" grass, most commonly rye. Nurse grass is quick to germinate in cool spring weather, provides the necessary protection for the slower-to-develop turf grasses, and typically dies out after the first season.

Fescue, the most shade-tolerant grass, has a fine thin leaf blade. Bluegrasses and perennial rye, in all their many varieties, have broader leaf blades and require more sun to flourish. While lawns do not generally thrive in full shade, a turf mix with a good percentage of fescue—often called a "sun and shade" mix—will establish better than a mix that relies primarily on bluegrass varieties, which will thin and die out in shady areas.

Ve·nus fly·trap: A carnivorous plant found only in the Carolinas and in strange plastic capsules in novelty stores.

Common Lawn Weeds

Weed	Type	Means of Spread
Annual Bluegrass	*Grassy, cool season annual*	Seed
Autumn Hawkbit	*Broadleaf, perennial*	Seed, reshoots from taproot
Bermudagrass	*Grassy, warm season perennial*	Stolon, rhizome
Bird's Foot Trefoil	*Broadleaf, perennial*	Rhizome
Cat's Ear	*Broadleaf, perennial*	Seed, reshoots from taproot
Chickweed	*Broadleaf, cool season annual*	Seed
Crabgrass	*Grassy, warm season annual*	Seed
Creeping Bentgrass	*Grassy, cool season perennial*	Seed, vigorous stolons
Creeping Buttercup	*Broadleaf, perennial*	Creeping rootstock
Dallisgrass	*Grassy, warm season perennial*	Seed, creeping rootstock
Dandelion	*Broadleaf, perennial*	Seed, reshoot from taproot
Dove's Foot Cranebill	*Broadleaf, perennial*	Seed, creeping runners
English Daisy	*Broadleaf, perennial*	Creeping stems
Field Wood Rush	*Grassy, perennial*	Seed
Foxtail	*Grassy, warm season annual*	Seed
Germander Speedwell	*Broadleaf, perennial*	Creeping rootstock
Goosegrass	*Grassy, warm season annual*	Seed
Ground Ivy	*Broadleaf, perennial*	Seed, rhizome
Henbit	*Broadleaf, cool season annual*	Seed, rooting stems
Knotweed	*Broadleaf, warm season annual*	Seed

Weed	Type	Means of Spread
Lesser Trefoil	*Broadleaf, annual*	Seed
Mouse Ear Chickweed	*Broadleaf, perennial*	Seed, creeping stems
Mouse Ear Hawkweed	*Broadleaf, perennial*	Creeping runners
Nimblewill	*Broadleaf, perennial*	Seed, stolon
Nutgrass	*Grassy, perennial*	Seed, rhizome, small tubers
Orchardgrass	*Grassy, cool season perennial*	Seed
Pearlwort	*Broadleaf, perennial*	Seed, rooting stems
Purslane	*Broadleaf, warm season annual*	Seed
Quackgrass	*Grassy, cool season perennial*	Seed, rhizome
Roughstalk Bluegrass	*Grassy, cool season perennial*	Seed, stolon
Selfheal	*Broadleaf, perennial*	Creeping runners
Sheep Sorrel	*Broadleaf, perennial*	Seed, creeping rootstock
Spear Thistle	*Broadleaf, biennial*	Seed
Spotted Medick	*Broadleaf, perennial*	Seed
Tall Fescue	*Grassy, cool season perennial*	Seed
White Clover	*Broadleaf, perennial*	Seed, creeping rootstock
Yarrow	*Broadleaf, perennial*	Stolon
Yellow Sorrel	*Broadleaf, perennial*	Seed

Controls

Perennial grassy weeds, especially those that spread by stolon or rhizome, are best dealt with by the tedious chore of lifting and sifting out their roots from existing turf and border plantings.

Broadleaf weeds can quickly establish and spread in thinning turf. The best control is to cultivate and maintain a healthy, vigorous lawn that will not allow these pests to gain a foothold. Physically remove existing weeds of this sort in cool, damp spring weather when the soil is easy to work. The application of an herbicide, organic or not, is most effective when done in the fall, when the plants are storing energy in their root systems for the winter and will draw the control down into their root systems, quickly killing them.

Any control of annual weeds must be applied before the plants flower and set seed, creating another season of weeding headaches.

Tonic Tea for Haggard Houseplants

Watering houseplants with hard water can inhibit uptake of soil nutrients, the result being a pale and undernourished appearance. One tablespoon of apple cider vinegar added to each gallon with every watering will shift the pH into the neutral range and restore proper nutrient uptake.

Raw, unpasteurized apple cider vinegar contains many trace minerals and, used properly, will quickly green up ailing houseplants and serve as a general tonic. On the other hand, the application of straight vinegar (10 percent acidity) directly on the foliage of any plant will kill it outright.

Basic Backyard Compost

1 part green material: Lawn clippings, kitchen scraps, garden gleanings. Fresh moist organic material provides nitrogen and moisture.

1 part brown material: Dried leaves, small twigs, straw, sawdust, shredded newspaper, coffee grounds. Dried, fibrous material provides carbon and texture, and allows for good air circulation.

1 part black material: Garden soil, manure, and/or existing unfinished compost all provide the matrix for the decomposition of the other two components as well as introduce valuable soil organisms necessary to that process.

Do not include: Pet wastes (potential to spread disease); diseased plant clippings (ditto); meat (attracts undesirable wildlife and will stink as it decays); inorganic materials such as plastic, glass, aluminum, and so on.

Slug-Be-Gone Vanishing Spray

1½ cups non-sudsing ammonia
1½ cups water

Combine ammonia and water in a 1-quart spray bottle. Spray in areas where slug damage is evident early in the season. The solution will dissolve baby slugs on contact, while the ammonia will break down into a form of nitrogen and feed the plants—a win–win situation for all but the slug.

Therapeutic Qualities of Essential Oils

Bee balm (aka bergamot)	Uplifting, cleansing, antidepressant
Eucalyptus	Invigorating, antiseptic, decongestant, analgesic
Grapefruit	Bright, uplifting, cleansing, stimulating
Lavender	Antifungal, antiseptic, antidepressant, calming, deodorizing, antibacterial
Lemon	Energizing, antiseptic, astringent, antibacterial
Sweet orange	Uplifting, antispasmodic, balancing, antiseptic
Peppermint	Stimulating, refreshing, uplifting, cooling, antiseptic, expectorant
Rose	Sensual, antidepressant, tonic, astringent, antispasmodic, sedative
Rosemary	Warming, stimulating, analgesic, antiseptic, antispasmodic, astringent
Sandalwood	Soothing, sensual, centering, antiseptic, sedative, warming
Thyme	Antibacterial, warming, stimulating, expectorant

Nutrient Roles in Plant Nutrition

Primary Nutrients

Nutrient	Symptoms of Deficiency
Nitrogen (N)	Yellowing leaves with stunted growth
Phosphorus (P)	Leaves take on a red or purple cast along with stunted growth
Potassium (K)	Leaf tips and margins yellow, then brown, along with weakening stems

Careful observation of a plant's appearance together with a soil analysis will identify deficiencies of these three primary nutrients. Correct any imbalance with soil amendments and fertilizers.

Secondary Nutrients
Sulfur, calcium, magnesium

Micronutrients
Iron, molybdenum, manganese, zinc, chlorine, boron, copper, nickel

Deficiencies of secondary and micronutrients will manifest with some or all of the following symptoms: leaves yellow but veins remain green, growth is stunted, plant tissues may thicken and disfigure while buds and young leaves die back from the tip. These shortages are best treated collectively with a micronutrient fertilizer rather than for individual imbalances.

How to Conduct a Home Soil pH Test

Soil pH determines a plant's ability to absorb nutrients. When it's too high or too low, the nutrients in the soil become locked up and unavailable. On the pH scale 7 is neutral, less than 7 is acid, and more than 7 is alkaline. Most plants prefer a fairly neutral soil. To sweeten a sour or acid soil, incorporate agricultural lime to raise the pH. To balance an alkaline soil, incorporate sulfur or cottonseed meal to lower the pH toward neutral.

Our agrarian ancestors, as well as the most down-to-earth gardeners of today, would conduct a simple taste test of their soil to check its' pH. An acid soil tastes and smells sour. A more reliable method, and less of an assault on the palate, is to place a soil sample into a jar of vinegar. If the vinegar bubbles the soil is sweet, and planting may commence; an absence of bubbles indicates a sour or acid soil, which must be sweetened before planting. Or, you can purchase a soil pH test kit from a local nursery, complete with highly detailed instructions, a vial containing a reagent, and a color-coded chart calibrated to measure the results.

Plants requiring sweet soil: asparagus, baby's breath, beets, bergenia, broccoli, cabbage, cauliflower, chard, clematis, coral bells, cosmos, elm, hawthorn, iris, Japanese anemone, lavender, leeks, lilac, locust, melon mulleins, nasturtiums, onions, peonies, phlox, pinks, rosemary, rue, snapdragons, spinach, sweet peas, thyme, zinnia.

Plants requiring acid soil: apple, azalea, birch, bleeding heart, blueberries, brambleberries, butterfly weed, camellia, candytuft, carrots, dogwood, eggplant, euphorbia, gardenia, heaths and heather, holly, juniper, lupine, parsley, pine, potato, pumpkin, rhododendron, tomato.

Culinary Herbs and Food Matches

Anise/fennel	Cheeses, sweets, fruit, fish, salads, sauces
Basil	Cheeses, fish, fruit, salads, sauces, soups, stews, vegetables, eggs, rice/pasta
Bay leaf	Beef, soups, rice/pasta
Chervil	Cheeses, fish, salads, sauces, vegetables, eggs, rice/pasta
Chive	Beef, cheeses, salads, sauces, vegetables, eggs
Dill	Breads, cheeses, fish, salads, sauces, stews, vegetables, eggs, rice/pasta
Garlic	Beef, breads, cheeses, lamb, pork, rice/pasta
Lemon verbena	Cakes, fruit, tea
Marjoram	Beef, breads, cheeses, lamb, salads, sauces, soups, vegetables, rice/pasta
Mint	Fruit, lamb, salads
Oregano	Breads, cheeses, lamb, poultry, salads, sauces, rice/pasta
Parsley	Cheeses, fish, pork, salads, soups, stews, vegetables, eggs
Rose geranium	Sweets, fruit
Rosemary	Beef, breads, lamb, pork, poultry, sauces, rice/pasta
Sage	Cheeses, pork, poultry, stews
Sorrel	Fish, salads, sauces, vegetables, eggs, rice/pasta
Tarragon	Fish, salads, sauces, soups, vegetables, eggs
Thyme	Breads, cheeses, fish, lamb, pork, poultry, vegetables, eggs

Mojito

4–6 mint leaves
Juice of 1 lime
1 teaspoon powdered sugar
2 ounces white rum
Club soda

Muddle the first three ingredients together in a pint glass. Fill with crushed ice and add the rum. Strain into a serving glass, top with club soda, and garnish with a sprig of mint. Today's mojito is a descendant of a much older drink called the "draquecito" (the little dragon), named for Sir Francis Drake, the infamous pirate who plundered the Caribbean in the sixteenth century.

Mint Julep

1 lump sugar
1 tablespoon water
4 sprigs fresh mint
2 ounces bourbon

Muddle the first three ingredients together in a tall glass or traditional silver tumbler. Fill with crushed ice, add bourbon, and serve without stirring.

Common Toxic Garden Plants

Plant	Toxic Parts and Symptoms
Autumn crocus	Bulb—gastrointestinal; possibly fatal
Azalea	All parts—gastrointestinal, neurological, respiratory; fatal
Belladonna	Young plants, seeds—digestive, muscular; fatal
Black locust	All parts—gastrointestinal, neurological, cardiac; possibly fatal
Bleeding heart	Foliage, roots—neurological, muscular
Bloodroot	All parts—respiratory, visual; possibly fatal
Bouncing Bet	Seeds—burning in mouth, gastrointestinal
Buttercup	All parts—digestive system injury
Cardinal flower	All parts—cardiac, gastrointestinal; possibly fatal
Castor bean	Seeds, foliage—neurological, burning in mouth; fatal
Cherry	Twigs, foliage—respiratory, neurological
Cherry laurel	All parts—gastrointestinal, neurological, respiratory
Christmas rose	All parts—gastrointestinal, cardiac; possibly fatal
Clover	Leaves—gastrointestinal
Daffodil	Bulb—gastrointestinal; possibly fatal
Daphne	Berries—gastrointestinal burning; fatal
Delphinium	Young plants, seed—digestive, muscular; fatal
Dutchman's-breeches	All parts—neurological, respiratory
Elderberry	Roots—gastrointestinal
English holly	Berries—severe gastrointestinal
English ivy	Foliage, berries—digestive, respiratory, possible coma
Foxglove	Leaves, seed, flowers—cardiac, digestive, neurological
Horse chestnut	Fruit—gastrointestinal, neurological; possibly fatal
Hyacinth	Bulb—gastrointestinal; possibly fatal

Plant	Toxic Parts and Symptoms
Hydrangea	Bud, foliage, wood—gastrointestinal, respiratory
Iris	Fresh roots/tubers—moderate gastrointestinal
Jack-in-the-pulpit	All parts—intense burning in mouth
Larkspur	Young plants, seed—gastrointestinal, muscular; fatal
Lily of the valley	Foliage, flowers—cardiac, digestive, neurological; fatal
Mayapple	All parts—gastrointestinal
Milkweed	Leaves, fruits, stems—cardiac, respiratory, gastrointestinal
Mistletoe	All parts, especially the berries—fatal
Monkshood	All parts—gastrointestinal, neurological; possibly fatal
Morning glory	All parts—severe neurological in large amounts; fatal
Nightshade	All parts—severe gastrointestinal, neurological; possibly fatal
Oak	Foliage, acorns—gradual renal failure
Oleander	All parts—digestive, cardiac, contact burns; fatal
Poinsettia	All parts—gastrointestinal; possibly fatal
Pokeweed	All parts—gastrointestinal
Poppy	Foliage, roots—neurological, muscular
Potato	Foliage—gastrointestinal, neurological
Privet	Berries, foliage—digestive; possibly fatal
Rhododendron	All parts—gastrointestinal, neurological, respiratory; fatal
Rhubarb	Foliage—renal, neurological; possibly fatal
Snowdrop	Bulb—digestive, neurological
Star of Bethlehem	Bulb, flowers—gastrointestinal, neurological
Sweet pea	Seed—gastrointestinal
Tomato	Vines—digestive, neurological
Wisteria	Seed—digestive
Yew	Leaves, seed, twigs—full body involved; fatal

Gardeners on the Go on the East Coast

Rocky Hill, CT: Dinosaur Sate Park Arboretum. Of special interest for budding paleontologists is the Arboretum of Evolution, featuring 250 species and cultivars of conifers as well as ginkgo, katsuras, magnolias, and other plants that can trace their roots back to when dinosaurs roamed the Earth.

Appledore Island, ME: Celia Thaxter's Garden. This nineteenth-century re-creation of a traditional cottage garden as described in Thaxter's book, *An Island Garden*, is based on the book's charming illustrations by Childe Hassam. Once a week the garden, set on a rocky island devoid of paved roads or walkways, is open to tourists who arrive by boat from nearby Seabrook, NH.

Portsmouth, RI: Green Animals Topiary Garden. What began as a garden folly by a nineteenth-century cotton tycoon with an accomplished Portuguese gardener is now one of America's oldest and best-loved topiary gardens. Covering a 7-acre estate overlooking Narragansett Bay, the garden features eighty elaborately clipped topiaries, twenty-one of which are the "green animals" that give the garden its name.

Provincetown, MA: Day's Cottages. Humble two-bedroom vacation cottages form a single line along the Atlantic shore. The twenty-three identical cottages, identified simply by the name of a flower, are clad in white clapboard with deep forest green shutters and window trim. Cottages 1 through 24 (with no cottage number 13) are named as follows: Daisy, Phlox, Poppy, Aster, Rose, Lilac, Tulip, Peony, Violet, Crocus, Dahlia, Zinnia, Cosmos, Iris, Salvia,

Petunia, Begonia, Larkspur, Bluebell, Marigold, Primrose, Wisteria, and Arbutus.

Iselin, NJ: Garden for the Blind and Disabled. This circular sensory garden located outside the Iselin Public Library was constructed in 1974 and consists of a waist-high bricked-in raised bed containing various plants chosen for their textural qualities and fragrance over their visual impact.

Bronx, NY: Wave Hill. This 28-acre public garden and cultural center overlooking the Hudson River is home to some of the most acclaimed gardens in the country. For the specialist at heart, the Monocot garden contains only plants that produce a single seed leaf upon germination. From this narrow constraint, luxuriant gardens have been created around banana trees, taro, all sorts of grasses and grains, as well as lilies, cannas, and day lilies.

Virginia Beach, VA: Mount Trashmore Park. The first landfill park in the world was first opened to the public in 1973. This park, a favorite among locals and tourists alike, was built on the site of a 125-acre landfill. At 60-some feet above sea level, it is the highest point in the region, serving as a visual reminder of a community's commitment to environmental awareness.

State Flowers, Birds, and Trees

State	Flower	Bird	Tree
Alabama	Camellia	Yellowhammer	Longleaf pine
Alaska	Forget-me-not	Willow ptarmigan	Sitka spruce
Arizona	Saguaro cactus	Cactus wren	Paloverde
Arkansas	Apple blossom	Mockingbird	Loblolly pine
California	California poppy	California Valley quail	California redwood
Colorado	Blue columbine	Lark bunting	Colorado blue spruce
Connecticut	Mountain laurel	American robin	White oak
Delaware	Peach blossom	Blue hen chicken	American holly
District of Columbia	'American Beauty' rose	Wood thrush	Scarlet oak
Florida	Orange blossom	Mockingbird	Sabal palm
Georgia	Cherokee rose	Brown thrasher	Live oak
Hawaii	Hibiscus	Nene	Candlenut
Idaho	Lilac	Mountain bluebird	Western white pine
Illinois	Violet	Cardinal	White oak
Indiana	Peony	Cardinal	Tulip tree
Iowa	Wild rose	Goldfinch	Oak
Kansas	Sunflower	Western meadowlark	Cottonwood
Kentucky	Goldenrod	Kentucky cardinal	Tulip poplar
Louisiana	Magnolia	Eastern brown pelican	Bald cypress
Maine	Pinecone	Chickadee	Eastern white pine
Maryland	Black-eyed Susan	Baltimore oriole	White oak
Massachusetts	Mayflower	Chickadee	American elm
Michigan	Apple blossom	American robin	Eastern white pine
Minnesota	Showy ladyslipper	Common loon	Red pine

State	Flower	Bird	Tree
Mississippi	Magnolia	Mockingbird	Magnolia
Missouri	Hawthorn	Bluebird	Flowering dogwood
Montana	Bitteroot	Western meadowlark	Ponderosa pine
Nebraska	Goldenrod	Meadowlark	Cottonwood
Nevada	Sagebrush	Mountain bluebird	Single-leaf pinyon pine
New Hampshire	Lilac	Purple finch	White birch
New Jersey	Purple violet	Eastern goldfinch	Northwestern red oak
New Mexico	Yucca	Roadrunner	Pinyon pine
New York	Rose	Bluebird	Sugar maple
North Carolina	Dogwood	Cardinal	Longleaf pine
North Dakota	Wild prairie rose	Western meadowlark	American elm
Ohio	Scarlet carnation	Cardinal	Buckeye
Oklahoma	Mistletoe	Scissor-tailed flycatcher	Redbud
Oregon	Oregon grape	Western meadowlark	Douglas fir
Pennsylvania	Mountain laurel	Ruffed grouse	Eastern hemlock
Rhode Island	Purple violet	Rhode Island hen	Red maple
South Carolina	Carolina jessamine	Carolina wren	Sabel palm
South Dakota	Pasqueflower	Pheasant	Black hills spruce
Tennessee	Iris	Mockingbird	Tulip poplar
Texas	Bluebonnet	Mockingbird	Pecan
Utah	Sego lily	California seagull	Blue spruce
Vermont	Red clover	Thrush	Sugar maple
Virginia	Flowering dogwood	Cardinal	Flowering maple
Washington	Rhododendron	Willow goldfinch	Western hemlock
West Virginia	Flowering dogwood	Cardinal	Sugar maple
Wisconsin	Wood violet	Robin	Sugar maple
Wyoming	Indian paintbrush	Meadowlark	Plains cottonwood

Cleansing Room Spray

6 ounces distilled water in a glass bottle with a spray
   top
12 drops lavender oil
12 drops eucalyptus oil
12 drops bergamot oil
100 drops of essential oil emulsifier (optional)

Add the essential oils to the water (use only high-quality, pure essential oils). Shake well to mix and mist room lightly. Great for clearing the air of a sickroom during cold and flu season.

Other useful blends: A blend of rosemary, grapefruit, geranium, tea tree, and patchouli essential oils can reduce the effect of harmful chemicals given off by cigarette smoke, cleaning solutions, and the off-gassing of new carpets and draperies; well employed in office environments. To deodorize the kitchen of cooking smells, combine eucalyptus, rosemary, lavender, and grapefruit essentials oils.

Relief from Tension Headaches and Stress

15 drops lavender oil
10 drops peppermint oil
½ ounce almond oil

Combine all and store in a dark stoppered bottle. Apply this cool, soothing mixture to temples and forehead at first indication of pain.

Gardener's Balm

¼ cup almond oil
¼ cup olive oil
¼ cup grated beeswax
15 drops lavender oil
10 drops juniper oil
10 drops clove oil
10 drops cinnamon oil

Heat oils until hot and stir in beeswax to melt completely. Allow to cool to nearly room temperature before blending in essential oils. Stir thoroughly and pour into small jars to store. Makes a protective treatment for chapped and garden-worn hands.

Aromatherapy

Aromatherapy is the study and use of the healing properties of fragrant plants, primarily through the distillation and use of essential oils that concentrate a particular plant's benefits.

To Ease	Try
Aggression	Bergamot, chamomile, juniper, lemon, marjoram, rosemary, ylang-ylang
Anger	Chamomile, jasmine, marjoram, rose, rosemary, ylang-ylang
Anxiety	Bergamot, chamomile, geranium (for balance), lavender, neroli, orange, patchouli, rose (for confidence), sandalwood, sweet marjoram, vetiver (for grounding)

To Ease	Try
Disappointment	Bergamot, cypress, jasmine, orange, rose
Fear	Cedarwood, fennel, ginger, patchouli, sandalwood, thyme
Grief	Bergamot, chamomile, jasmine, marjoram, neroli, rose
Hysteria	Chamomile, lavender, neroli, orange, tea tree
Impatience	Chamomile, clary sage, frankincense, lavender
Indecision	Basil, clary sage, cypress, jasmine, patchouli, peppermint
Jealousy	Jasmine, rose
Fatigue (emotional and mental)	Basil, cardamom, clary sage, cinnamon leaf or bark, clove bud, coriander, eucalyptus, ginger, grapefruit, jasmine, juniper, orange, peppermint, rosemary, thyme, vetiver, ylang-ylang
Fatigue (physical)	Basil, ginger, lemon, lavender, orange, peppermint, rosemary
Nervousness	Chamomile, clary sage, coriander, frankincense, neroli, orange, vetiver
Panic	Chamomile, clary sage, geranium, jasmine, juniper, lavender, neroli, ylang-ylang
Sadness	Jasmine, rose, rosewood
Shock	Lavender, neroli, rose, tea tree
Shyness	Black pepper, ginger, jasmine, neroli, patchouli, peppermint, rose, ylang-ylang
Stress	Bergamot, cedarwood, Roman chamomile, all citrus oils, clary sage, geranium, lavender, sweet marjoram, melissa, neroli, patchouli, petitgrain, rose, rosemary, sandalwood, vetiver, ylang-ylang
Suspicion	Jasmine, lavender
Tension	Chamomile, clary sage, cypress, geranium, jasmine, lavender, lemon, marjoram, neroli, orange, rose, rosewood, sandalwood, ylang-ylang

Breathe Yourself Young Again

The sense of smell is said to be the most direct link between the world and that part of our brain that encapsulates memory. The philosopher Jean Jacques Rousseau wrote, "Smell is the sense of the imagination."

A whiff of freshly mown grass and you are 6 years old again, rolling down the neighbors' front lawn, screaming with abandon and not a care in the world. Coumarin, an essence that embodies the smell of freshly mown grass, is in many essential oils—not bad for a 5-minute vacation from responsibilities, deadlines, and pressure.

Chic Greens in Your Backyard

Considered common weeds by many, the following plants also find their way into gourmet herbal salad mixes and are sold for top dollar at finer markets:

- *Chickweed (Stellaria media):* Annual. Rich in copper, making for a nutritious as well as delicious cress in salads and sandwiches.
- *Corn salad (Valerianella locusta):* Annual. Rich and buttery salad green having a somewhat nutty flavor.
- *Dandelion (Taraxacum officinale):* Perennial. Harvest young leaves to include in spring salads. Mature leaves may be

stewed as pot greens, while the mature roots, when roasted to a dark brown in a warm oven, may be ground and brewed to create a healthful coffee substitute.

❧ *Fiddleheads:* Primarily gathered from the ostrich fern (*Matteuccia struthiopteris*). Perennial, although other emerging ferns may be harvested if picked when tightly coiled. Reminiscent of the flavor of asparagus and a good source of vitamins A and C.

❧ *Garlic mustard (Allium alliaria):* Biennial. Harvest shoots and leaves for their mild garlic flavor. Ripe seeds lend a peppery punch to dishes, while the mature root may be used in the same manner as horseradish.

❧ *Plantain (Plantago):* Perennial. Prepare leaves fresh or cooked, as you might spinach.

❧ *Stinging nettle (Urtica dioica):* Perennial. Makes a nutritious tea and a valuable pot green.

❧ *Wild dock (Rumex spp.):* Perennial. A relative of domestic rhubarb having a lemony, sour flavor. Harvest stalks and leaves.

❧ *Wild leeks or ramps (Allium tricoccum):* Bulb. Use the whole plant, including the bulb, raw in spring salads or cooked as you would a mild leek.

❧ *Wood sorrel (Oxalis acetosella):* Perennial. Young leaves make a tartly delicious addition to tonic spring salad or a flavorful sauce for fish.

The Good and the Bad—They're All Ugly

Bacteria are microscopic single-celled organisms that are classified near the bottom of the plant kingdom. Bacterial diseases, while similar in symptoms to fungal diseases, are absent the fruiting bodies and spores present in the latter. Control measures call for the removal and destruction of the affected plants, as these diseases are difficult to treat. Precaution against infection is the gardener's best defense.

Good Bacteria	Bad Bacteria
Help to break down soil additives to make them available to plants	Blight and wilt
Fix nitrogen in the soil	Rot
Displace harmful bacteria	Promote leaf spot
Are critical in the fermentation process of various nutrient or compost teas, resulting in a "live" soil additive said to inoculate the garden with the listed benefits of good bacteria	Promote galls and scab

Sexual Propagation

Sexual propagation is dependant on seeds that result from the mixing of genetic material between two parent plants through the process of pollination. This method is the most common form of reproduction among plants and ensures constantly evolving genetic diversity.

Asexual Propagation

Asexual propagation involves growing tissue from an existing plant to produce a duplicate or clone of that particular plant. This method is employed in the propagation of hybrid plants, which would not come "true" from seed or which might be sterile and not produce viable seed. Asexual propagation also ensures a uniform crop and a predictable outcome, generally the goal in a commercial application.

Examples of Asexual Propagation

Cuttings: The removal of a piece of the parent plant (stem, leaf, or root) to produce an entirely new complete copy of the plant. This is possible because individual plant cells are able to duplicate all plant parts and functions.

Layering methods: Causing roots to form along shoots that are still attached to the parent plant. The stem is not removed from the main plant until roots are fully formed.

Grafting or bud grafting: Joining together different parts of two different plants. Fruit trees are often grafts, with the fruiting part of the plant joined to a different rootstock to control hardiness, growth, and eventual size of the mature tree.

Division: Cutting or gently teasing apart a plant crown or cluster of shoots into separate pieces, preferably taken from the younger and more vigorous growth around the perimeter of the clump. Each piece must have a growth bud and some roots to successfully grow into an identical replica of the parent plant.

Micropropagation or tissue culture: Employs the ability of individual plant cells to regrow an entire plant from a single cell. Under specialized laboratory conditions a small portion of a parent plant can be manipulated to create huge numbers of single cells that will all grow into exact copies of the parent plant. This has proved a huge boon to commercial horticulture, as it enables creating volumes of plant material to order. On the other hand, this method is generally only available to larger corporations with access to specialized equipment, not to mention funding, making it difficult for the small specialty grower to compete when introducing new plants to the trade.

Asparagus (*Asparagus officinalis*)

- A long-lived perennial characterized by edible green spears that emerge in early spring.
- While a well-prepared mature asparagus bed is capable of producing for 15 years without replanting, initially each plant must be tended for 2–3 years before harvesting to allow the rootstock to build strength.
- Common pests and diseases include the asparagus beetle, rust, Fusarium wilt, and crown rot. Various organic controls are available, though healthy and vigorous plants are resistant to pests and infection.
- Fat and cholesterol free and naturally low in sodium, asparagus is one of the most nutrient-dense vegetables available.

- *Oven-roasted:* Preheat oven to 450°. Snap woody ends from fresh asparagus and discard. Place remaining shoots on a sturdy sheet pan. Drizzle with olive oil and sprinkle with fresh, coarsely ground pepper and sea salt. Roast 10–15 minutes until lightly browned, shaking pan halfway through cooking period to turn spears. Remove from oven and serve with a squeeze of fresh orange juice and garnished with finely grated orange zest.

- *Wines* with a crisp acidity and flavors of citrus, grass, and mineral best compliment asparagus dishes. Pair asparagus with a medium-dry white wine such as chenin blanc or sauvignon blanc (fumé blanc).

The U.S. Department of Agriculture

The USDA is an administrative branch of the federal government. First established in 1862, its work is to administrate, regulate, investigate, and inform the agricultural community at large, as well as the home gardener, on all things gardening and agricultural. This work is carried out under the direction of the secretary of agriculture, an appointed cabinet position.

Corinthian Columns

Developed during the Hellenistic period (330 BC–first century AD), Corinthian columns introduced the notion of purely decorative elements to architectural forms. The capitols are patterned after the decorative foliage of *Acanthus* plants, or bear's breeches, a large perennial known for its glossy lobed foliage.

Cutting Garden

A cutting garden is an area of the garden managed similarly to cultivated vegetable crops but for producing cut flowers for home and market. Some suitable plants for cutting follow.

Winter/Spring

Shrubs
Camellia (*Camellia japonica* or *C. sasanqua*)
Forsythia (*Forsythia intermedia*)
Heather/heath (*Calluna/Erica*)
Lilac (*Syringa vulgaris*)
Pussy willow (*Salix*)
Quince (*Chaenomeles*)
Red-twig dogwood (*Cornus alba*)
Rhododendron/azalea (*Rhododendron*)
Winter daphne (*Daphne odora*)
Winter hazel (*Corylopsis*)
Witch hazel (*Hamamelis*)

Bulbs
Daffodil (*Narcissus*)
Hyacinth (*Hyacinthus*)
Tulip (*Tulipa*)
Many minor bulbs

Perennials
Bleeding heart (*Dicentra*)
Foxglove (*Digitalis purpurea*)
Fumitory (*Corydalis*)
Lungwort (*Pulmonaria*)
Primrose (*Primula*)
Spurge (*Euphorbia*)
Violet (*Viola*)
Wallflower (*Cheiranthus* or *Erysimum*)

Summer

Shrubs
Brambles (*Rubus*)
Butterfly bush (*Buddleia*)
Hydrangea (*Hydrangea*)
Lavender (*Lavandula*)
Rose (*Rosa*)
Tree mallow (*Lavatera*)

Bulbs
Begonia (*Begonia*)
Crocosmia (*Crocosmia*)
Dahlia (*Dahlia*)
Gladiolus (*Gladiolus*)
Iris (*Iris*)
Lily (*Lilium*)

Ornamental onion (*Allium*)
Peacock orchid (*Acidanthera*)

Perennials

Artemisia foliage
Aster (*Aster*)
Beardtongue (*Penstemon*)
Bee balm (*Monarda*)
Black-eyed Susan (*Rudbeckia hirta*)
Cape fuchsia (*Phygelius*)
Catmint (*Nepeta*)
Delphinium (*Delphinium*)
Hosta foliage
Japanese Anemone (*Anemone* x*hybrida*)
Ornamental sage (*Salvia*)
Peruvian lily (*Alstromeria*)
Phlox (*Phlox*)
Many, many more—select for long stems and ease of
cultivation

Annuals

Bachelor's button (*Centaurea cyanus*)
Bells of Ireland (*Molucella laevis*)
Calendula (*Calendula*)
Clarkia (*Clarkia or Godetia*)
Cosmos (*Cosmos*)
Flowering tobacco (*Nicotiana*)
Larkspur (*Consolida*)
Love-in-a-mist (*Nigella damascena*)
Marigold (*Tagetes*)
Mexican sunflower (*Tithonia*)
Nasturtium (*Tropaeolum*)

Ornamental corn (*Zea mays*)
Poppy (*Papaver*)
Salpiglossis (*Salpiglossis*)
Scabiosa (*Scabiosa*)
Snapdragon (*Antirrhinum*)
Sunflower (*Helianthus*)
Sweet pea (*Lathyrus odoratus*)
Sweet William (*Dianthus barbatus*)
Zinnia (*Zinnia*)

A Familiar Guest at Picnics

Ants, a common garden insect and a familiar guest at picnics, have
a well-developed social organization consisting of a queen and
her workers. Hatched from eggs, the majority of the resulting
larvae will be sterile workers intent solely on caring for the
queen as well as gathering and managing food sources. A small
percentage will hatch to become winged males and females; after
mating the male dies while the female will fly to a suitable nest
location to lay her eggs and raise subsequent generations.

Gardeners on the Go in the South

Coconut Creek, FL: Busch Gardens. Don't miss Butterfly World,
an 8,000-square-foot tropical rain forest aviary filled with exotic
blooms, waterfalls, and tropical plants dazzling with 5,000 exotic
butterflies.

Frankfort, KY: The Floral Clock. This 34-foot-diameter planter bedded out with more than 10,000 plants to represent the face of a clock is a truly operational timepiece weighing more than 200,000 pounds elevated over a reflecting pool. Each year visitors toss thousands of dollars in coins into the pool, which is handed over to child and welfare agencies statewide, proving once again that time in the garden is never wasted.

Raleigh, NC: Juniper Level Botanic Gardens. Informal plantings of beautifully grown plants arranged in bold, artful displays serve as a test garden for Plant Delights Nursery and illustrate the potential impact of the many small containerized plants available on nursery sales tables. Renowned for its hosta breeding and selection, Plant Delights is home to hundreds of hosta introductions, including the fabulously named 'Elvis Lives', 'Dixie Chick', 'Hillbilly Blues', and 'Squash Casserole'.

Oracle, AZ: Biosphere 2 Center. A 7-million-cubic-foot glass structure containing five different wilderness ecosystems—desert, savanna, rain forest, ocean, and marsh—as well as agroforestry and human habitat.

Gaffney, SC: The Peachoid. Agricultural pride was manifest in 1980 when the Gaffney Board of Public Works commissioned a 1-million-gallon water tower in the shape of a giant peach to promote South Carolina's production of the sweet fruit. What the board did not anticipate were the traffic snarls caused by the completed water tower, visible from nearby I-85 and said to bear an uncanny resemblance to a giant, naked rear end.

Nashville, TN: The Opreyland Hotel. This enormous plantation-style hotel boasts 9 acres of climate-controlled, indoor gardens within its system of massive atriums. Visitors board flat-bottomed boats to cruise the (also indoor) river, saving what must amount to thousands of dollars on sunscreen and bug repellant.

Summerville, GA: Paradise Gardens Park and Museum. Occupying 2½ acres of reclaimed wetlands, Paradise Gardens is the creation of Reverend Howard Finster, who began his career as a bicycle repairman and went on to become one of America's most well known folk artists for his quirky, two-dimensional art pieces as well as his spiritual ramblings. The garden was part and parcel of the reverend's largely self-taught ministry and home to many of his early paintings as well as the various shards of glass, abandoned autos, and salvaged materials he used to adorn the site in a unique vision of color and creative energy. Finster passed on in 2001, leaving a legacy of more than 46,000 works of art in addition to the garden, which has begun to fade and slip back into the swamp.

ar·bo·re·tum: A collection of live trees and woody plants used for scientific and educational research.

Top U.S. Arboretums

Arnold Arboretum of Harvard University, Boston, MA
Bartlett Arboretum and Gardens, Stamford, CT
Dawes Arboretum, Newark, OH
Holden Arboretum, Kirtland, OH
JC Ralston Arboretum, Raleigh, NC
Morton Arboretum, Lisle, IL
Planting Fields Arboretum State Historic Park, Oyster Bay, NY
Strybing Arboretum, San Francisco, CA
University of California at Davis Arboretum, Davis, CA
U.S. National Arboretum, Washington DC

an·nu·al: A plant that grows from seed to maturity, flowers, sets seed, and dies within a single year.

bi·en·ni·al: A plant that grows from seed, taking 2 years to reach maturity. The first year, foliage and roots develop, followed by flowers, seed production, and death in the second year.

pe·ren·nial: A plant that continues to grow year after year, sending up foliage and flowers that die back with the onset of winter only to return again the following season from the rootstock.

e·ter·nal: A plant or flower often fashioned of silk or a cheaper synthetic fabric. While some highly detailed and accurate representations exist, these faux plants generally fool no one.

Best in Show

Perhaps the most prestigious plant trial and awards program is that of England's Royal Horticultural Society. Each year, following extensive garden trials and evaluations by learned horticulturalists, promising plants are bestowed with an Award of Garden Merit (AGM).

On this side of the pond, the All-American Selections (AAS) was created for registering, testing, scoring, and promoting interesting new flowers and vegetables through a network of trial grounds established throughout the country, where "worthy" seed varieties are field-grown "blind," identified only by a number. At the close of the season, judges within the program score their evaluations and select those varieties deemed exceptional garden performers, identifying them as AAS Winners. Trials have continued every year since 1932, making AAS the oldest, most established testing organization in North America.

The First AAS Winners, 1933

Flowers

'Annual Mixed' Canterbury bell
'Beauty of Oxford Hybrids' verbena
'Cambridge Blue' delphinium
'Dwarf Swiss Giants' pansy
'Giant King Mixed' lupine
'Golden Gleam' nasturtium

'Guinea Gold' marigold
'Lavender Glory' verbena
Venidium fastuosum

Vegetables

'Asegrow Stringless Black Valentine' snap bean
'Asegrow Stringless Green Pod' snap bean
'Clark's Special' cucumber
'Giant Nobel' spinach
'Graystone' watermelon
'Honey Rock' cantaloupe
'Imperator' carrot
'Improved Profecto' cantaloupe
'Ohio Canner' beet
'Pritchard' tomato

American Rose Society

Founded in 1892, the American Rose Society (ARS) is an educational, nonprofit organization dedicated to furthering the cultivation and enjoyment of the rose. Biannual competitions governed by strict standards and guidelines award recognition to roses raised by ARS members that are deemed excellent. A generous thirty-six named awards are granted to outstanding entries each year.

Run for the Roses

Red roses became the official flower of the Kentucky Derby in 1904. The phrase "Run for the Roses" is attributed to Bill Corum, a New York sportswriter who became president of Churchill Downs, where this most recognized horse race has been held since 1875. The winning horse receives a green satin garland containing 554 red roses. The highlight is the "Crown," a single rose pointing upward in the center of the garland, a metaphor for "the struggle and heart necessary to reach the winner's circle." The winning jockey also receives a bouquet of five-dozen long-stemmed roses presented by the Kentucky governor.

Gardeners on the Go out West

Vail, CO: Get high at the Betty Ford Alpine Gardens. At 8,200 feet above sea level, the world's highest botanic garden is internationally recognized for its dramatic display of high-elevation plants set in the midst of Rocky Mountain grandeur.

Green River, UT: The World's Largest Watermelon. A giant motorized melon was created more than 50 years ago to celebrate the town's annual Watermelon Days festival. While no longer motorized, the "giant slice on wheels" is still hauled out of storage, given a fresh coat of paint, and paraded through town each August.

Sequim, WA: Annual Lavender Festival. In a state better known for its gray skies and drizzle, it is a heady delight to come upon acres and acres of lavender fields in full bloom. Sheltered by the rain shadow of the Olympic Mountains, the area is home to nearly thirty lavender farms where every third week of July the fragrant harvest is celebrated with tours, U-pick fields, lavender products, and delicious regional cuisine.

Big Trees

ℵ

Let every tree lover, every forester, every lumberman rally . . . to fight for the preservation of our biggest tree specimens.

—JOSEPH STEARNS, FORESTER (1940)

Since 1940, the American Forests' National Register of Big Trees has documented and recorded the largest known specimens of every native and naturalized tree in the United States. Trees are measured in volume, with points awarded based on the following formula: trunk circumference (in inches) + height (in feet) + ¼ average crown spread (in feet). The largest tree within each species countrywide is designated a national champion.

The General Sherman Tree, a giant sequoia (*Sequoiadendron giganteum*) in Sequoia National Park, California, is considered the largest tree in the world:

Height above base. . . . . *274.9 feet*
Circumference at ground level . . . . *102.6 feet*
Diameter of largest branch . . . . *6.8 feet*
Average crown spread . . . . *106.5 feet*

The World's Smallest Park

Located in Portland, Oregon, the park was the creation of
Dick Fagan, a journalist whose office at the *Oregon Journal*
overlooked a busy street as well as a hole in the median strip
originally intended for a light pole. Fagan cleaned up the site,
planted flowers, and officially dedicated it as "the world's smallest
park," being a mere 24 inches in diameter and only 452 square
inches in area. Fagan, a proud Irishman, dedicated the park on
Saint Patrick's Day in 1948, naming the park Mill Ends after
his column of the same name. Until his death in 1969, Fagan
continued to describe the park and its various activities, claiming
it to be the only leprechaun colony west of Ireland. Portland
Parks and Recreation acquired Mill Ends in 1976. The park was
relocated briefly in 2006 to accommodate construction on the
nearby parkway before returning to a new and permanent home
just 7½ feet from its original location at SW Naito Parkway and
Taylor Street.

The Garden State

New Jersey was first referred to as the Garden State by the
honorable Abraham Browning of Camden, New Jersey, at the
Centennial Exhibition in Philadelphia on New Jersey Day,
August 24, 1876. Mr. Browning extolled the agricultural riches of
the state that over time had fed the soldiers of the Revolutionary
War as well as provided for the tables of the good citizens of New
Jersey, New York, and Pennsylvania. In 1954 the state legislature
voted to add the legend "Garden State" to New Jersey license
plates over the protests of then-governor Alfred E. Driscoll, who
believed it too narrow a moniker to represent the many valuable
industries and occupations of modern-day New Jersey.

Weight of Wood

Cedar is the lightest landscape timber, weighing in at 22 pounds
per square foot. White oak is twice as heavy at 45 pounds per
square foot.

Scofield Heat Units

A system devised in 1912 by an American pharmacist named
Wilber Scofield to measure the heat of garden chiles or peppers.
The test measures the amount of sugar that has to be dissolved

into a cup of water before the capsaicin, the "heat" element present in peppers, no longer affects the palate. A panel of volunteers was seated to test the system—there is no record as to how these brave palates fared, but the hottest peppers, such as the habanero or Scotch bonnet, scored 100,000–300,000 Scofield units, while the somewhat milder jalapeño scored a mere 2,500–4,000 units. Bell peppers scored nothing at all.

Tobacco Mosaic Virus

The longest word in English is the name for the tobacco mosaic virus:

acetylseryltyrosylserylisoleucylthreonylserylprolylserylglutaminyl-phenylalanylvalylphenylalanylleucylserylserylvalyltryptophylalanyl-aspartylprolylisoleucylglutamylleucylleucylasparaginylvalylcysteinyl-threonylserylserylleucylglycylasparaginylglutaminylphenylalanyl-glutaminylthreonylglutaminylglutaminylalanylarginylthreonyl-threonylglutaminylvalylglutaminylglutaminylphenylalanylserylglu-taminylvalyltryptophyllysylprolylphenylalanylprolylglutaminyls-erylthreonylvalylarginylphenylalanylprolylglycylaspartylvalyltyro-syllysylvalyltyrosylarginyltyrosylasparaginylalanylvalylleucylaspar-tylprolylleucylisoleucylthreonylalanylleucylleucylglycylthreonyl-phenylalanylaspartylthreonylarginylasparaginylarginylisoleucyliso-leucylglutamylvalylglutamylasparaginylglutaminylglutaminylser-ylprolylthreonylthreonylalanylglutamylthreonylleucylaspartylala-nylthreonylarginylarginylvalylaspartylaspartylalanylthreonylvalylal-anylisoleucylarginylserylalanylasparaginylisoleucylasparaginyl-

leucylvalylasparaginylglutamylleucylvalylarginylglycylthreonylgly-
cylleucyltyrosylasparaginylglutaminylasparaginylthreonylphenyl-
alanylglutamylserylmethionylserylglycylleucylvalyltryptophylthrco-
nylserylalanylprolylalanylserine

Sissinghurst's White Garden

Often referred to as the most copied garden in the world,
Sissinghurst's white garden by Vita Sackville-West and her
husband, Harold Nicholson, includes the following plants:

Maidenhair fern (*Adiantum pedatum*)
Pacific chrysanthemum (*Ajania pacifica*)
White-flowered ornamental onion (*Allium carinatum* ssp.
   pulchellum 'Album')
German garlic (*Allium senescens*)
White snapdragon (*Antirrhinum*)
'Nivea' columbine (*Aquilegia vulgaris* 'Nivea')
'Quinta White' daisy (*Argyranthemum* 'Quinta White')
Southernwood (*Artemesia abrotanum*)
'Lambrook Silver' wormwood (*Artemesia absinthium*
   'Lambrook Silver')
Roman wormwood (*Artemesia pontica*)
Mugwort (*Artemisia alba* 'Canescens')
'Powis Castle' wormwood (*A.* 'Powis Castle')
Smooth heath aster (*Aster pilosus* var. *demotus*)
White rock rose (*Cistus* x*cyprius*)
Clematis forsteri
'John Huxtable' clematis (*Clematis* 'John Huxtable')

Naked lady (aka white autumn crocus) (*Colchicum specisoum* 'Album')
'White Sensation' cosmos (*Cosmos bipinnatus* 'White Sensation')
Ornamental sea kale (*Crambe cordifolia*)
'Musgrave's Pink' pink (*Dianthus* 'Musgrave's Pink')
Blue lyme grass (*Elymus arenarius*)
Euphorbia altissima
Double-flowered queen of the meadow (*Filipendula ulmaria* 'Flore Pleno')
White goats rue (*Galega* xhartlandii 'Alba')
White-flowered meadow cranesbill (*Geranium pratense* ssp. *pratense* f. *albiflorum*)
Bowman's root (*Gillenia trifoliata*)
Green-flowered tobacco (*Nicotiana alata* 'Lime Green')
'Little Diamond' English ivy (*Hedera helix* 'Little Diamond')
'Shamrock' English ivy (*Hedera helix* 'Shamrock')
Licorice plant (*Helichrysum petiolare*)
'Royal Standard' hosta (*Hosta* 'Royal Standard')
'Sazanami' hosta (*Hosta crispula* 'Sazanami')
Oriental iris (*Iris orientalis*)
'White Swirl' Siberian iris (*Iris sibirica* 'White Swirl')
'Flying Squadron' iris (*Iris* 'Flying Squadron')
Springblossom (*Jaborosa integrifolia*)
White-flowered everlasting pea (*Lathyrus latifolius* 'Albus')
Giant daisy (*Leucanthemella serotina*)
Shasta daisy (*Leucanthemum* xsuperbum)
'Noble Maiden' lupine (*Lupinus* 'Noble Maiden')
Plume poppy (*Macleaya cordata*)
White-flowered musk mallow (*Malva moschata* 'Alba')
South African honey bush (*Melianthus major*)
White-flowered love-in-a-mist (*Nigella* 'Album')

Scotch thistle (*Onopordum acanthium*)
'Cheddar Gold' peony (*Paeonia lactiflora* 'Cheddar Gold')
'Ivory Jewel' peony (*Paeonia lactiflora* 'Ivory Jewel')
'White Wings' peony (*Paeonia lactiflora* 'White Wings')
'Abbotswood' shrubby cinquefoil (*Potentilla* 'Abbotswood')
Mulligan climbing rose (*Rosa mulliganii*)
'Double White' Scotch rose (*Rosa pimpinellifolia* 'Double White')
'Iceberg' rose (*Rosa* 'Iceberg')
'White Wings' rose (*Rosa* 'White Wings')
Silver sage (*Salvia argentea*)
'Miss Wilmott' pincushion flower (*Scabiosa* 'Miss Wilmott')
White-flowered potato vine (*Solanum jasminoides* 'Album')
'Rowallane' feverfew (*Tanacetum parthenium* 'Rowallane')
Silver lace chrysanthemum (*Tanacetum ptarmiciflorum*)
'White Cloud' meadow rue (*Thalictrum aquilegifolium* 'White Cloud')
White-flowered Yunnan meadow rue (*Thalictrum delavayi* 'Album')
White-flowered Culver's root (*Veronicastrum virginicum* 'Album')
White cleome (*Cleome hasslerana*)
White four-o'-clock (*Mirabilis jalapa*)
White verbena (*Verbena novalis*)
'Crowborough' calla lily (*Zantedeschia aethiopica* 'Crowborough')

Plants in Space

Stuart Roosa, an astronaut on the Apollo 14 NASA mission to orbit the moon, was a former smokejumper for the U.S. Forest Service. The astronauts were allowed to bring a small collection of personal items, and Roosa chose several different kinds of tree seeds—a connection with his former occupation. After the mission the Forest Service planted the seeds to see if their exposure to microgravity would affect their growth. The seedlings thrived and the Forest Service ended up with hundreds of "Moon Trees." The seedlings were distributed to organizations around the country and many of the mature trees still survive.

The Ever-Present Aster

Believing asters to be composed of stardust and therefore sacred, the ancient Romans planted these hardy perennials surrounding their temples to honor the gods. The French placed asters on the graves of fallen soldiers to honor bravery and valor. Today these flowers, with their characteristic daisylike blooms, have naturalized throughout the world and can be found in meadows, salt marshes, mountainsides, and prairies with a bloom period among the various species that spans from early spring through late fall.

Quincunx

Quincunx spacing is defined as five objects arranged so that four are at the corner of a square or rectangle and the fifth at its center—for example, the sides of dice that show five or a five in a suit of cards. This term was introduced by learned Englishmen in the seventeenth century. Such object placement has historically been employed when setting out orchards, bedding schemes, and groundcovers.

How to Make a Rose Emoticon

@]->--

Good to Know . . .

Parsley has long been considered an antidote to poison. Historically, the placement of a sprig of parsley on a guest's plate indicated that no poison was intentionally added to the meal.

Christopher Lloyd (1921-2006)

A lion of English horticulture, Lloyd was known to keep several of his awards from the Royal Horticultural Society thumbtacked in his chicken coop turned retail center at Great Dixter.

Rock Me

In stone-scaping terminology, "one-man rock" refers to the number of men it would take to place a given stone using an 8-foot bar as a lever; given human variability, the range may be from quite small up to 300 pounds. A "two-man rock" can weigh upward of 900 pounds.

More Stone-Scaping Terminology

Rubble: Uncut stone suitable for stepping stones or masonry veneers.

Flagstone: Any stone what can be split into shallow slabs suitable for patio paving, stepping stones, and masonry veneers.

Landscape rock: Natural boulders suitable for walls, water-feature elements, edging, and outcroppings.

Columnar basalt: Naturally occurring, typically hexagonal column forms suitable for upright elements, entryway monuments, water-source stones, and small retaining walls.

Dimensional rock: Regularly cut stone suitable for formal paving and masonry veneers.

Cobbles or setts: Cut natural stone approximating the size of a large brick suitable for paving and edging.

River rock: Naturally rounded stones from 1 to 6 inches suitable for groundcover and landscaping applications as well as a component used in exposed aggregate.

Crushed stone: Mechanically formed "gravel," graded by size, suitable for walkways, groundcover, and setting larger pavers.

cu·bic yard: A unit of volume used to measure sand, gravel, and other landscaping materials.

  ❦ *1 cubic yard covers 324 square feet 1 inch deep.*

  ❦ *1 cubic yard covers 162 square feet 2 inches deep.*

  ❦ *1 cubic yard covers 108 square feet 3 inches deep.*

  ❦ *1 cubic yard covers 81 square feet 4 inches deep.*

  ❦ *1 cubic yard covers 54 square feet 5 inches deep.*

"Don't think I haven't tried; I have fertilized my crops with a variety of stimulants. I have scatted Hitler's speeches and most of DuPont's most expensive chemicals over their stunted growths, but so far all I have to show for my trouble is a small bed of wild marijuana, a spring of mint, and a dislocation of the trunk muscles that has an excellent chance of developing into a full-blown rupture . . . I only hope that Uncle Sam isn't relying too heavily on my Victory Crop to sustain the nation through the coming winter."

—GROUCHO MARX (1895–1977), AMERICAN COMEDIAN

America's Favorite Daylilies

The American Hemerocallis Society sponsors an annual popularity poll to determine which daylily is the most popular. An award is presented in each of the following regions:

Region 1 *North Dakota, South Dakota, Nebraska, Minnesota, Iowa, and Manitoba, Canada*

Region 2 *Wisconsin, Illinois, Indiana, Michigan, Ohio*

Region 3 *Kansas, Oklahoma, Missouri, Pennsylvania, New Jersey, Maryland, Delaware, Washington DC, West Virginia, Virginia*

Region 4 *Maine, Vermont, New Hampshire, New York, Massachusetts, Rhode Island, Connecticut, and Canada's Newfoundland, Labrador, Prince Edward Island, Nova Scotia, New Brunswick, Quebec, and Ontario*

Region 5 *Georgia*

Region 6 *New Mexico, Texas*

Region 7 *California, Nevada, Arizona, Hawaii*

Region 8 *Washington, Oregon, Alaska, and Canada's Yukon, Northwest Territories, Nunavut, and British Columbia*

Region 9 *Montana, Idaho, Wyoming, Utah, Colorado, and Canada's Alberta and Saskatchewan*

Region 10 *Kentucky, Tennessee*

Region 11 *Kansas, Oklahoma, Missouri*

Region 12 *Florida*

Region 13 *Arkansas, Louisiana*

Region 14 *Mississippi, Alabama*

Region 15 *North Carolina, South Carolina*

Fibonacci

Leonardo Fibonacci was a thirteenth-century Italian mathematician known for his number theories. A Fibonacci number is a number in a series in which each number is a sum of the previous two entries; for example, 0, 1, 1, 2, 3, 5, 8, 13, 21, 34, 55, 89, 144, 233, 377, 610, 987.... Throughout nature many petals, seeds, leaves, and branching patterns are arranged in spirals that reflect Fibonacci number sequences. The thinking is that this structure forms the most efficient and optimal arrangement of seeds, petals, and so on, allowing equal sun exposure and room for each plant part to develop.

Flowery Mead

A common garden type prevalent in late medieval times, composed of a grassy area spotted with naturalized plantings of meadow flowers such as English daisies, primroses, forget-me-nots, violets, daffodils, cowslips, wild strawberries, and cornflowers.

Plants Mentioned in the Writings of Shakespeare

Plants of literate and symbolic reality: Aloe, anemone, ash, bay, birch, borage, box, broom, calendula, caraway, chamomile, columbine, crocus, cuckoo flower, cupid's-dart, daisy, daylily, dogwood, elder, English daisy, fennel, flax, garlic, geranium, hawthorn, hemlock, holly, hyacinth, hyssop, lavender, lemon, mallow, mandrake, marigold, monkshood, moss, nettle, oak, olive, palm, pansy, parsley, peony, pine, pinks, poppy, primrose, quince, rose, rosemary, rue, saffron, sage, santolina, spurge, tarragon, thyme, yarrow, yew, violet.

Lawn Furniture

1. Select an area in the garden that receives at least 6 hours of sun a day. Because this "furniture" will not be portable, attention should be given to traffic patterns and other design considerations.
2. Remove any existing plantings in your selected area and outline the shape of your finished seating area.
3. Create a structural armature for the seat using cement breeze blocks and boards, filling the resulting form with dampened soil, tamping it firmly into place as you go.
4. Lay sod over the form, pressing it firmly into contact with the underlying soil and working to define the shape of the seat. Hold sod in place with landscape staples until roots form to anchor the planting.
5. Water regularly and trim to maintain shape.

Gardeners on the Go in the Heartland

Chicago, IL: The Winter Garden. Housed on the ninth floor of the Harold Washington Library Center, the world's largest public library. The building itself is crowned with magnificent botanical ornaments and figures to represent wisdom and the power of the life force: vines, twining leafs, seedpods, and enormous owls measuring 75 feet tall and 40 feet wide. The lush garden is glass-roofed and filled with potted olive trees and climbing plants, providing an antidote to Chi-town's notoriously harsh winters.

Des Moines, IA: Arie den Boer Arboretum. From the end of each April through the middle of May the arboretum is a flurry of rosy petals when the world's largest collection of flowering crab apple trees is in bloom. To honor the memory of a family member or friend, you can make a modest donation and a tree will be planted, adding to the spectacle of this growing collection.

Atchison, KS: The International Forest of Friendship. Established in 1976 by the Ninety-Nines, an international organization of women pilots, to honor and commemorate their founding president, Amelia Earhart. On significant occasions honoring contributors to the history of aviation, flags of thirty-five countries fly in a forest of trees from all fifty states and the represented countries.

Saint Louis, MO: The Jewel Box Conservatory. This striking Art Deco style conservatory built in 1936 is listed on the National Historic Register as an outstanding example of greenhouse design. In addition to its permanent plant collection, six times a year fabulous seasonal floral and plant displays are mounted to much public acclaim.

Ashippun, WI: Honey of a Museum. A small museum associated with Honey Acres, a large honey producing operation, is filled with fun facts, sweet trivia, and honey-producing implements and offers an array of tempting samples.

Sidney, NE: Living Memorial Gardens. In a clever repurposing move by local citizens, a 1940s public swimming pool in Legion Park was turned into a sunken garden commemorating loved ones and their contributions to the community. The same site is also home to a 141-foot flagpole and one of the country's largest American flags.

Columbus, OH: Topiary Gardens. In this unique interpretation of life imitating art, fifty-four topiary specimens have been created in a tableaux of Georges Seurat's famous post-Impressionist painting, *A Sunday Afternoon on the Island of La Grande Jatte.*

Common Corn

Cornflowers, corn cockles, and corn poppies are just a few plants with "corn" in their common names that are in no way related to edible corn. Early Europeans referred to all grains as "corn," passing this name along to the many self-sowing flowers that would establish in fields under cultivation.

Oh Tanenbaum

- *Top Christmas tree–producing states:* California, Oregon, Michigan, Washington, Wisconsin, Pennsylvania, and North Carolina.
- *Ready for harvest:* Six to ten years at approximately 6 to 7 feet. Almost all trees require shearing to attain the traditional Christmas-tree shape.
- *The use of evergreen trees* to celebrate the winter season occurred before the birth of Christ.
- *An acre of Christmas trees* provides for the daily oxygen requirements of eighteen people.

Popular Christmas Tree Varieties

Arizona cypress
Balsam fir
Canaan fir
Colorado blue spruce
Concolor fir
Douglas fir
Eastern red cedar
Eastern white pine
Fraser fir
Grand fir
Leyland cypress
Noble fir
Norway spruce
Scotch pine
Virginia pine
White spruce

White House National Christmas Trees

Year	Christmas Tree	Living/Cut
1924–29	35' Norway spruce	Living
1929–30	Norway spruce	Living
1931–33	25' blue spruce	Living
1934–38	23' fir	Living
1939	32' red cedar	Living
1940	32' red cedar	Living
1941–53	Two 30' Oriental spruces planted side by side, decorated in alternate years	Living
1954	67' balsam fir	Cut
1955	65' white spruce	Cut
1956	67' Engelmann spruce	Cut
1957	60' white spruce	Cut
1958	74' Engelmann spruce	Cut
1959	70' white spruce	Cut
1960	75' Douglas fir	Cut
1961	75' Douglas fir	Cut
1962	72' blue spruce	Cut
1963	71' Norway spruce	Cut
1964	72' Adirondack white spruce	Cut
1965	70' blue spruce	Cut
1966	65' red fir	Cut
1967	70' balsam fir	Cut
1968	74' Engelmann spruce	Cut
1969	75' Norway spruce	Cut
1970	78' spruce	Cut
1971	63' Fraser fir	Cut
1972–76	42' Colorado blue spruce	Living
1977	34' Colorado blue spruce	Cut
1978–present	30' Colorado blue spruce	Living

State	President
New York	Coolidge, Hoover
New York	Hoover
Washington DC	Hoover, Roosevelt
North Carolina	Roosevelt
Virginia	Roosevelt
Virginia	Roosevelt
Relocated from White House grounds	Roosevelt, Truman, Eisenhower
Michigan	Eisenhower
South Dakota	Eisenhower
New Mexico	Eisenhower
Minnesota	Eisenhower
Montana	Eisenhower
Maine	Eisenhower
Oregon	Eisenhower
Washington	Kennedy
Colorado	Kennedy
West Virginia	Johnson
New York	Johnson
White Mountain Apache Indian Reservation, Arizona	Johnson
California	Johnson
Vermont	Johnson
Utah	Johnson
New York	Nixon
South Dakota	Nixon
North Carolina	Nixon
Pennsylvania	Nixon, Ford
Maryland	Carter
Pennsylvania	Carter, Reagan, George H. W. Bush, Clinton, George W. Bush

Windchill Factor

		Temperature (Fahrenheit)							
		35	**30**	**25**	**20**	**15**	**10**	**5**	**0**
Wind Speed (mph)	**5**	31	25	19	13	7	1	-5	-11
	10	27	21	15	9	3	-4	-10	-16
	15	25	19	13	6	0	-7	-13	-19
	20	24	17	11	4	-2	-9	-15	-22
	25	23	16	9	3	-4	-11	-17	-24
	30	22	15	8	1	-5	-12	-19	-26
	35	21	14	7	0	-7	-14	-21	-27

ha–ha: A sunken ditch faced with a masonry retaining wall or fence encircling a property. The ha-ha allows a view to flow from a domesticated landscape smoothly into surrounding parkland while preventing cattle and other livestock from entering the public grounds.

Types of Tomatoes

Determinate: Bush-type plants that grow to a certain size, stop, and set all their fruit at once.

Indeterminate: Vining-type plants that continue to grow and produce fruit throughout the season.

Patio: Plants that are specifically bred to be small enough to grow in a window box or container.

Heirloom: Generally said to be nonhybrid tomatoes that have been grown for generations. Known for their exceptional flavor, rich color, and heady aroma, heirloom tomatoes have endured because of careful cultivation and the seed-saving skills of generations of gardeners throughout the world.

Hybrid: Plants that have been developed to be more disease resistant and uniform in production for large-scale food processing—in some, but not all, cases at the expense of true tomato flavor.

Tomato Varieties

Cultivar Name	Type	Days to Harvest	Growth Habit
'Alicante'	Salad	70	Indeterminate
'Amish Paste'	Salad	74	Indeterminate
'Aunt Ruby's'	Slicing	80	Indeterminate
'Banana Legs'	Roma	75	Determinate
'Big Beef'	Slicing	70	Indeterminate
'Black Krim'	Slicing	70	Indeterminate
'Black Plum'	Salad	75	Indeterminate
'Black Prince'	Slicing	70	Indeterminate
'Brandywine'	Slicing	85	Indeterminate
'Camp Joy'	Cherry	65–70	Indeterminate
'Carmello'	Slicing	70	Indeterminate
'Caspian Pink'	Slicing	75	Indeterminate
'Celebrity'	Slicing	70	Determinate
'Cherokee Purple'	Slicing	75	Determinate
'Clear Pink'	Slicing	65–70	Determinate
'Cosmonaut Volkov'	Slicing	65	Indeterminate
'Costoluto Genovese'	Slicing	78	Indeterminate
'Dona'	Slicing	75	Indeterminate
'Early Cascade'	Salad	70	Indeterminate
'Early Girl'	Slicing	62	Indeterminate
'Elfina'	Cherry	55	Determinate
'Garden Peach'	Salad	70	Indeterminate
'Gardener's Delight'	Cherry	70	Indeterminate
'German Red Strawberry'	Slicing	75	Indeterminate
'Gold Nuggets'	Cherry	60	Determinate
'Grape'	Cherry	55	Indeterminate
'Green Grape'	Cherry	65	Determinate

Heirloom	Description
Heirloom	1–2" firm, red fruit, English
Heirloom	8 oz. deep red fruit with a rich "real tomato" flavor
Heirloom	12–16 oz. green and pink fruit with a delicious spicy flavor
Heirloom	Yellow fruit on productive plants
	Large, round, red beefsteak with a full rich flavor
Heirloom	10–12 oz. deep purple, flavorful fruit, heavy producer
Heirloom	2" plum-shaped mahogany colored fruit
Heirloom	Medium-sized dark garnet fruit, Russian
Heirloom	Very large, to 7", deep pink fruit with a rich tomato flavor, Amish
	1–1½" flavorful red fruit on large productive plants
	3–4" red fruit with a good sweet/acid balance, very productive
Heirloom	Large pink, "brandywine" type fruit with good flavor
	7–8 oz. firm red fruit
	4" deep purple-pink fruit with a delicious flavor
Heirloom	2" meaty fruit with few seeds and a rich flavor, Russian
	8–12 oz. deep red, knobby fruit with a sweet rich flavor, Russian
Heirloom	Large, deeply lobed red fruit with a rich flavor, productive
Heirloom	Slightly flattened deep red fruit with a full flavor, French
	2" red fruit with a good acid balance
	4–6 oz. red fruit, consistent early producer
	Small red fruit produced on dwarf plants suitable for pot culture
Heirloom	3–4" pinky-yellow fruit with a wonderful tropical fruit flavor
Heirloom	Red, full flavored, crack resistant variety
Heirloom	10 oz. rich red strawberry-shaped fruit with dense flesh and great flavor
Heirloom	Bright yellow fruit produced on small plants suitable for pot culture
	Red oval fruit with good flavor
	Sweet tangy green fruit, bred for green catsup production

Cultivar Name	Type	Days to Harvest	Growth Habit
'Green Zebra'	Slicing	70	Determinate
'Grushovka'	Salad	70	Indeterminate
'Husky Gold'	Salad	70	Determinate
'Italian Gold'	Roma	70	Determinate
'Jaune Flamme'	Salad	60	Indeterminate
'Juliet'	Salad	60	Indeterminate
'Koralik'	Cherry	61	Determinate
'Legend'	Slicing	68	Determinate
'Lemon Boy'	Salad	75	Determinate
'Marglobe'	Salad	73	Determinate
'Marmande'	Slicing	68	Indeterminate
'Martina'	Salad	58	Indeterminate
'Matt's Wild Cherry'	Cherry	60	Indeterminate
'Micro-Tom'	Cherry	70	Determinate
'Money Maker'	Salad	77	Indeterminate
'Mortgage Lifter'	Slicing	75	Indeterminate
'Moskovich'	Slicing	60	Indeterminate
'Mr Stripey'	Salad	65	Indeterminate
'Nebraska Wedding'	Slicing	73	Indeterminate
'Northern Exposure'	Slicing	67	Determinate
'Old German'	Slicing	75	Indeterminate
'Oregon Spring'	Salad	55	Determinate
'Patio'	Salad	70	Determinate
'Pearly Pink'	Cherry	65	Indeterminate
'Persimmon'	Slicing	80	Indeterminate
'Polish Linguisa'	Salad	73	Indeterminate
'Principe Borghese'	Roma	75	Determinate

Heirloom	Description
	2–3 oz. green striped fruit flushes yellow when dead ripe, outstanding flavor
	Large, blocky dense red fruit
	7–8 oz. golden fruit with excellent flavor, very productive
	Golden orange fruit, good for making sauce
Heirloom	2" blushed orange fruit with exquisite flavor
	2" red fruit set in trusses, excellent for sauce or drying
Heirloom	1" red fruit set in clusters of 6–8, ripens early and all at once
	8oz. red fruit bred for disease resistance
	Firm, juicy butter-yellow fruit, very productive
Heirloom	Firm, red fruit on compact, disease-resistant plants, delicious
Heirloom	Large, red lobed fruit with good flavor, French
Heirloom	2–4 oz. fruit with a rich full flavor, German
Heirloom	Intensely sweet red fruit on vigorous vines, Mexican
	Tiny red fruit, novelty plant can be grown in a very small pot
Heirloom	2–2½" red, uniformly round, flavorful meaty fruit borne in clusters
Heirloom	Large, smooth skinned flavorful pink fruit
Heirloom	4–6 oz. red fruit, very early to mature, Siberian
	Quirky, orange and yellow striped fruit
Heirloom	Large meaty fruit, to 1 lb, are richly flavored with an orange skin and yellow flesh
	Large, red delicious fruit bred for cool, short seasons
Heirloom	Large yellow delicious fruit with red and pink stripes throughout, Mennonite
	3–5 oz. red fruit produced early, continuing throughout the summer
	3 oz. red fruit on productive 2´ plants
	Delicious pink fruit on productive vines
Heirloom	Very large, deep orange oval fruit with a delicious flavor
Heirloom	8–10 oz. sausage-shaped red fruit, very productive, Polish
Heirloom	Nearly seedless, red fruit bred for drying, Italian

Cultivar Name	Type	Days to Harvest	Growth Habit
'Prudens Purple'	Slicing	67	Indeterminate
'Red Currant'	Cherry	65	Indeterminate
'Reisentraube'	Cherry	75	Indeterminate
'Rose de Berne'	Slicing	80	Indeterminate
'Ruby Pearl'	Cherry	67	Indeterminate
'San Remo'	Roma	76	Indeterminate
'Siletz'	Slicing	60	Indeterminate
'Silvery Fir'	Salad	60	Determinate
'Soldacki'	Slicing	70–75	Indeterminate
'Stupendous'	Slicing	55	Indeterminate
'Stupice'	Salad	60–65	Indeterminate
'Sun Gold'	Cherry	60	Indeterminate
'Sweet Million'	Cherry	65–75	Indeterminate
'Sweetie'	Cherry	75	Determinate
'Tangella'	Salad	65	Indeterminate
'Taxi'	Slicing	65	Determinate
'Tigerella'	Salad	60	Indeterminate
'Tuscany'	Roma	75	Determinate
'Viva Italia'	Roma	80	Determinate
'Yellow Currant'	Cherry	70	Indeterminate
'Yellow Pear'	Cherry	70	Indeterminate

Heirloom	Description
Heirloom	Large, deep pink fruit with crimson flesh, delicious with a smooth texture
	Long sprays of tiny, sweet crisp fruit, South American
	Small red fruit borne in cluster of 20–40, German
Heirloom	Beautiful 5 oz. pink fruit with a sweet flavor, Swiss
	Beautiful clusters of ½" sweet, jewel-like fruit on prolific vines
	Fat, sausage-shaped irregular red fruit, bred for sauce and drying
	12–16 oz. full flavored red fruit with few seeds, good in cool seasons
	2" red fruit on attractive plants clothed with silvery, lace-like foliage
Heirloom	Dense pink fruit with outstanding flavor, Polish
	Sweetly flavored fruit, very tolerant of the cold
Heirloom	Early yield of tasty red fruit, Czech
	Bright orange 1" fruit with a sweet tropical fruit flavor
	1" sweet red fruit with disease and crack resistance
	Very sweet red fruit, suitable for pot culture
	2–3 oz. orange fruit with a tangy flavor, English
	Beautiful 4–5 oz bright yellow fruit on stocky vines
	2–3 oz. red fruit with orange stripes, juicy and flavorful, English
	Dense red fruit with a rich flavor, good for sauce or drying
	Red fruit with outstanding flavor, produced on vigorous disease-resistant vines
	Tiny yellow fruit produced in abundance
Heirloom	Lemon-yellow, pear-shaped fruit with a mild sweet flavor

Bloody Mary

Worcestershire sauce—the dark, thin, piquant table condiment—
is a key ingredient in a good Bloody Mary. Its famous-yet-secret
formula is said to include garlic, soy sauce, tamarind, onion,
molasses, lime, anchovies, vinegar, chile pepper, and other
seasonings.

> 1½ ounces vodka
> 3 ounces tomato juice
> ½ teaspoon Worcestershire sauce
> 2–3 drops Tabasco to taste

*Combine ingredients and serve over ice in a tall glass garnished with a
lime wedge, celery, salt, and black pepper.*

How to Establish a Backyard Wildlife Habitat

To enjoy the beauty, life, and authentic sense of nature wildlife
bring to an urban landscape, you must provide for the basic
needs of an animal:

- *Food (berries, seeds, insects, etc.)*
- *Water (birdbath, water feature, small pond or stream)*
- *Sheltering shrubs, trees, and ground areas to provide safety from
  predators, protection from inclement weather, and nesting sites*

Establish a diverse planting of trees, shrubs, and flowering plants
to attract the greatest number of animal and bird species. Space

groups of plants in clusters while still allowing for areas of open space, also taking care to create plantings with varied heights in order to provide structural diversity. Eliminate the use of chemicals and always consider the impact of pest and disease controls on resident wildlife, even when employing organic methods.

Perennials with an Extended Bloom Period

These perennials have a colorful bloom period of 10 weeks or more:

'Moonshine' yarrow (*Achillea*)
Sea pink (*Armeria maritima*)
'Monch' aster (*Aster frikartii* 'Monch')
Bellflower (*Campanula carpatica, C. portenschlagiana*)
Red valerian (*Centranthus ruber*)
Shasta daisy (*Chrysanthemum maximum*)
Tickseed (*Coreopsis*)
Yellow bleeding heart (*Corydalis lutea*)
Fringed bleeding heart (*Dicentra exima*)
Purple coneflower (*Echinacea purpurea*)
Blanketflower (*Gaillardia*)
Butterfly flower (*Gaura lindheimeri*)
Cranesbill (*Geranium sanguineum* var. *striatum*)
Greyleaf cranesbill (*Geranium cinereum*)
Baby's breath (*Gypsophila*)
'Stella d'Oro' daylily (*Hemerocallis* 'Stella d'Oro')
Candytuft (*Iberis sempervirens*)
Hollyhock (*Alcea*)

Bee balm (*Monarda*)
Catmint (*Nepeta cataria*)
Russian sage (*Perovskia atriciplifolia*)
Balloon flower (*Platycodon grandiflorum*)
Garden phlox (*Phlox paniculata*)
Black-eyed Susan (*Rudbeckia fulgida*)
Meadow sage (*Salvia nemerosa*)
Pincushion flower (*Scabiosa caucasica*)
Showy stonecrop (*Sedum telephium*)
Prairie mallow (*Sidalcea*)
Stokes' aster (*Stokesia laevis*)
Spiderwort (*Tradescantia*)
'Sunny Border Blue' speedwell (*Veronica* 'Sunny Border Blue')

"Good God. When I consider the melancholy fate of so many of botany's notaries, I am tempted to ask whether men are in their right mind who so desperately risk life and everything else through the love of collecting plants."

—CARL LINNAEUS, *Glory of the Scientist* (1737)

How Plant Collectors Died . . . or Almost Died

William Sherard (1659–1728): Considered one of the finest English botanists of his day, Sherard was tragically mistaken for a wolf and shot while botanizing.

John Lawson (1674–1711): Author of *New Voyage to Carolina*, detailing his discoveries in the backcountry of North Carolina, including plants and the culture of native Indians. Lawson was killed by the Tuscarora Indians, who stuck him all over with pitch pine splinters before setting him on fire.

Francis Masson (1714–1805): As the first plant collector for the Royal Botanic Gardens at Kew, Masson was responsible for introducing more than 400 species of new plants, focusing primarily on flowering perennials. In the course of his many travels he routinely risked life and limb: he was chased by escaped convicts in Africa, forced to fight against the French in Grenada, and captured by pirates. The exact circumstances of his death at age sixty-four are not known.

Thomas Nuttall (1786–1859): Explored much of what is today the United States alone and on foot, collecting and documenting flora and fauna. At one point Nuttall was earnestly botanizing, using his gun to dig up plants, when he was overtaken and defenseless during an Indian raid. He survived and today is recognized as one of America's great naturalists.

David Douglas (1789–1834): A Scottish plant collector for the Horticultural Society of London, Douglas discovered the Douglas fir (*Pseudotsuga menziesii*), the sugar pine (*Pinus lambertiana*), the Sitka spruce (*Picea sitchensis*), and many other conifers. In 1934, while collecting plants on Hawaii, he fell into a pit dug by the islanders to trap wild cattle and was gored to death by a wild bull already captured.

Richard Cunningham (1793–1835): Killed by Australian aborigines while under the employment of the Royal Botanic Gardens at Kew.

Père Jean Marie Delavay (1834–95): One of a group of French missionary/botanists who collected more plant specimens than souls while in China between the years 1886 and 1905. Delavay was responsible for a great many plant introductions, including the wingthorn rose (*Rosa sericea pteracantha*, syn. *R. omeiensis pteracantha*). Even after contracting the bubonic plague in 1888, Delavay continued botanizing until his death 7 years later.

Père Jean André Soulié: (1858–1905) Another of the French missionaries in China between 1886 and 1905, Soulié is attributed with discovering the butterfly bush (*Buddleia davidii*) before being shot in Tibet.

How to Tie Garden Knots

Plants suitable for use in a knot garden:

Dwarf boxwood (*Buxus sempervirens* 'Suffruticosa')
Germander (*Teucrium chamaedrys*)
Cotton lavender (*Santolina incana*)
Dwarf English lavender (*Lavandula angustifolia*)
Box-leaf euonymus (*Euonymus japonica* 'Microphylla')
Japanese holly (*Ilex crenata* 'Convexa')

When One Plant Loves Another Plant Very Much

Monoecious: Male and female reproductive structures (flowers or cones) are present on the same plant; for example, corn where the tassel is the male part and the ears are the female part. From the Greek word for "one household."

Dioecious: Reproductive structures (flowers or cones) of a single sex per plant, with some plants being female and some being male. The presence of both sexes is necessary for seed or fruit formation; for example, holly. From the Greek word for "two households."

Horticulture-Related Sports Teams

The Fighting Artichokes, Scottsdale Community College, Scottsdale, AZ
Banana Slugs, University of California at Santa Cruz, Santa Cruz, CA
Beetdiggers, Jordan High School, Midvale, UT
Hockaday Daisies, Hockaday Preparatory School, Dallas, TX
Earwigs, Dunn School, Los Olivos, CA
Fighting Grape Pickers, North East High School, North East, PA
Irrigators, Newell High School, Newell, SD
Moundbuilders, Southwestern College, Winfield, KS
The Fighting Okra, Delta State University, Cleveland, MS
Russetts, Shelley High School, Shelley, ID
The Violets, New York University, Manhattan, NY

How to Lay a Flagstone Pathway

1. Mark the edges of your intended pathway with string and stakes. A path that gently curves lends grace and will make the garden appear larger.

2. Excavate the soil within the pathway to a depth of 4 inches. Tamp or roll the soil to create an even level. Recheck depth and lay down a 2-inch layer of crushed gravel over the soil and tamp down firmly. Using a builder's level, check to make sure your base remains level and even.

3. Spread 1 inch of builder's sand on top of the gravel base; do not tamp down. Your flagstones will be set into this foundation.

4. Set your stones in place, moving them around until you have a pleasing arrangement in a manner similar to working a jigsaw puzzle. Larger stones should be placed in the center of the pathway where they will create firmer footing, while smaller stones may be placed to fill the edges and empty spaces between the larger stones. Tap each stone into place firmly with a rubber mallet. Check one more time for level, adjusting underlying sand to accommodate differences in the stones thicknesses. Flagstones should be about ½ inch above original ground level when seated.

5. To finish, sweep damp sand into the spaces between the stones to set.

Anatomy of an Arbor

Footing: The base upon which the columns or posts are set. Must be strong enough to support the weight of the finished structure and extend into the ground beyond the frost line.

Columns or posts: Vertical supports for the overhead structure must be at least 4 inches by 4 inches and generally not be any shorter that 6 feet 8 inches to provide adequate head clearance. Material may be wood or cast stone.

Beams: Horizontal elements that tie the posts together. For a span of up to 6 feet, use 2- by 6-inch lumber; for longer spans, 2- by 8-inch lumber must be used to prevent sagging.

Rafters: These sit perpendicular to the underlying beams and are spaced at intervals to provide support for plants and degrees of shade. An additional layer of crosspieces, placed perpendicular to the rafters and composed of lighter-weight lumber, will add extra support as well as a decorative element to the finished structure. Rafters that run east-west provide the most shade, while those that run north-south allow in more sun. Lumber that is 1 inch by 2 or 3 inches and set on edge provides more shade when the sun is at an angle in the morning and again in the late afternoon.

Safe Steps Ensure Secure Strides

Tread: The surface of a step where you place your foot.

Rise: The height or vertical distance between one tread and the next.

Ideally the depth of the tread plus twice the riser height should equal 25 to 27 inches. Though risers and tread dimension can vary, their relationship should remain the same. Risers should be no lower than 5 inches and no higher than 8 inches. Treads should never be smaller than 11 inches.

Wide treads with short risers encourage a slower pace through the garden, while steeper risers in proportion with narrow treads naturally speed a walker through an area.

In any given flight of stairs, the risers should remain uniform and consistent; treads may vary with topography.

Beds and Borders

Garden bed: A defined area within a space containing a collection of plants.

Bedding: Denotes plants that have been massed in patterns and color blocks designed for showy flower and foliage effect for a single season; one has "bedded-out" the garden. Victorians raised this concept to an art with the creation of carpet bedding in the late nineteenth century. Elaborate and intricate designs were executed, generally by a large gardening staff, to resemble a family coat of arms, detailed geometric designs, and other floral wonders. Today, the best example of this highly technical, expensive—and one might say tedious—form of gardening can be found in public gardens, in the landscapes surrounding government buildings, and in amusement parks.

Garden border: Traditionally a mix of perennials planted in a wide swath to border a path, fence, or wall. Put one on either side of the path and you have a double border, a practice taken to its height in twentieth-century English gardens.

Mixed border: A mixed planting of perennials, bulbs, trees, shrubs, and ephemeral annuals. A practice adopted by gardeners of late who have neither the time, energy, or staff necessary to maintain a pure perennial border. An added benefit to a garden composed of mixed borders is an extended period of interest while most perennials lie dormant for many months of the year.

Bamboo

Distinctive, graceful, atmospheric, and sometimes terrifying. These woody, evergreen perennials are members of the grass family and can be found in climates as diverse as the gardens they adorn; bamboos are native to cold mountainous regions as well as the hot, steamy tropics. Bamboos may form a knee-high groundcover or shoot to the height of giants, lending a definite vertical element to any garden composition. While their foliage is predominantly green, their stems (or culms) vary from green, coral, pink, gold, and black, to even a chalky blue.

All bamboos, classified as either clumping or running, grow from an underground rhizome that spreads laterally, and therein lies the terror. Clumping bamboos have rhizomes that spread moderately each year and then send up new stems; clumps slowly increase in diameter to create a beautiful focal point or container specimen. Running bamboos are possessed of vigorous rhizomes that rapidly colonize an area before they send up their culms to quickly form a grove. Not easily controlled, the rhizomes have been known to push through concrete, let alone take over all available garden space.

Clumping Bamboos

Bambusa multiplex cultivars: Mostly upright, some with colorful culms with growth 8 to 20 feet; hardy to 15°F/–9°C.

B. oldhamii: Upright, timber-type growth 25 to 40 feet; hardy to 15°F/–9°C.

Chusquea culeou: Upright to 20 feet; hardy to 20°F/–7°C.

Fargesia murielae: Upright, arching at top, growth 6 to 15 feet; hardy to –20°F/–28°C.

Otatea acuminata ssp. *aztecorum:* Upright 10 to 20 feet but gracefully drooping; hardy to 15°F/–9°C.

Running Bamboos

Phyllostachys aurea: Upright and dense growth 10 to 20 feet, aggressive; hardy to 0°F/–18°C.

P. nigra: Upright growth 8 to 15 feet, culms turn black in second year; hardy to 0°F/–18°C.

P. vivax: Giant timber-type with growth to 50 feet; hardy to –5°F/–20°C.

Pleioblastus variegata: Rapid-spreading groundcover type with growth to 2 feet, green leaves are edged in white; hardy to 5°F/–15°C.

Semiarundinaria fastuosa: Upright growth 10 to 25 feet, moderate spreader; hardy to –5°F/–20°C.

Birdhousing 101

Only those birds that nest in tree hollows and other cavities will take up residence in a birdhouse. These include bluebirds, chickadees, nuthatches, swallows, and wrens. The type of house installed will determine, to a degree, which kind of bird will nest.

Small birds like chickadees, nuthatches, and most wrens prefer an entrance hole that is 1⅛ inches across. Medium-sized birds like bluebirds and swallows need a nest box with a hole that measures 1½ inches; white-breasted nuthatches need 1¼ inches. Tree swallows and violet-green swallows accept a wider variety of habitats and will often steal a nesting site from another bird. Larger birds such as purple martins and flickers require a 2¼- to 2½-inch opening.

Birdhouses should be constructed of materials that insulate well, such as 1-inch lumber, thick concrete, or heavy-walled clay vessels. Cheap plastic and novelty tin birdhouses, while lending a decorative note, are too thin and have poor ventilation; heat buildup can bake chicks inside or cause them to fledge prematurely.

Site a birdhouse with its entrance facing away from prevailing winds, and position it so that the young birds are safe from predators, for example atop a tall pole or hung from a branch of a tree. Place birdhouses away from any birdfeeders, as the constant activity surrounding the feeding station will unsettle the nesting birds.

A removable side panel or top is necessary so that the nesting box can be cleaned. Drainage holes in the bottom and ventilation holes on the sides will further keep the nesting bird in comfort. If you want more than one birdhouse, separate them by a considerable distance and out of sight of one another for nesting privacy.

Compost Coverage

Area to cover	2 inches deep	3 inches deep	4 inches deep
100 square feet	⅔ cubic yard	1 cubic yard	1⅓ cubic yards
250 square feet	1⅔ cubic yards	2½ cubic yards	3⅓ cubic yards
500 square feet	3⅓ cubic yards	5 cubic yards	6⅔ cubic yards
1,000 square feet	6⅔ cubic yards	10 cubic yards	13⅓ cubic yards

Note: A small pickup truck holds about 1 cubic yard, a full-sized pickup about 1½ cubic yards.

Degrees of Shade

Partial shade: During the course of a day, parts of the garden are exposed to direct sun for a period of time while residing in shade for at least half the day.

Filtered or dappled shade: Sunlight passing through a tree canopy or arbor will form a pattern of light and shade. A very pleasant and hospitable degree of shade for both plants and people.

Light or open shade: Bright, even shade in an open garden that is shaded by tall neighboring trees or buildings.

Full or deep shade: Little or no direct sunlight penetrates, as in a stand of dense evergreen trees. A challenging shade to garden with.

A Rose Is a Rose Is a Rose . . .

Climber: A shrub rose taller than 6 feet with flexible canes suitable for tying to supports.

Tall shrub: A shrub rose growing up to 6 feet or more.

Semivigorous shrub: A shrub rose growing up to 6 feet.

Low shrub: A shrub rose growing up to 3 feet.

Groundcover: Procumbent or ground-hugging rose shrubs.

Old Roses

Old or antique roses are generally held to be those roses that have been in cultivation for more than 100 years.

🌢 *Gallica (Rosa gallica):* Believed to be the rose of twelfth-century Persia as well as the 'Apothecary's Rose' of early France. Flowers are generally flat, are double, and have the unique property of retaining their color and fragrance when dried. Prune to replace the oldest wood with strong, young growth that will bear the best blossoms.

🌢 *Damask (R. damascena):* Believed to have originated in ancient Egypt, was traded throughout the civilized world by the Greeks between 800 and 600 BC, and was spread throughout Europe by the Romans during the Crusades. Damask roses were responsible for the development of the rose industry in Bulgaria in an area known as the Valley of Roses. Flowers once in summer; prune after flowering to shape and renew growth.

🌢 *Alba (R. alba):* This family of roses flower in a pale color range of cream, pink, rose, blush, and white, all having a delicious fragrance on vigorous hardy shrubs. So vigorous are these roses that they benefit from being cut back each season after flowering in an effort to control growth as well as renew the plant.

🌢 *Centifolia (R. centifolia):* Roses having 60 to 100 petals mentioned by historians who wrote in 410 BC of Midas's gardens are assumed to be the centifolia rose, now commonly referred to as the cabbage rose for their extremely doubled flower forms. Flowers bloom once a year on long, lax canes. Prune after flowering by shortening these canes by one half.

❧ *Moss rose:* Appearing first in Holland sometime around the year 1700, mutations of *R. centifolia* resulted in plants with prominent mosslike growth along the flower stems and at the base of the blooms. Considered a highly prized novelty, moss roses sold for exorbitant sums. Strongly fragrant flowers bloom once a year.

❧ *China (R. chinensis):* Roses introduced to Europe from China caused a quiet revolution with their recurrent blooms as well as the introduction of yellow to the color range. While China roses are not as popular as other types, their contribution to the rose world cannot be overstated.

❧ *Portland:* When it appeared in the middle of the nineteenth century, this rose caused great excitement for its habit of blooming several times a year, a trait not previously seen in garden roses. These roses, bearing fragrant, fully double blooms on very short stems, played a part in the parentage of the recurrent-blooming Hybrid Perpetuals and modern roses.

❧ *Bourbon:* Believed to be a natural cross between *R. damascena* and *R. chinensis*, this family of roses is known and valued for its compact growth, strongly fragrant pink blooms, and free-flowering habit.

al·le·lo·path·ic: Derived from the Greek word *allelon*, which means "reciprocally," and *pathos*, which means "to suffer." Plants with allelopathic tendencies release chemicals either through their roots or by means of their leaf litter that inhibit the growth or germination of plants growing nearby—in essence, a type of chemical competition.

Allelopathic Plants/Materials:

Black walnut tree
Broccoli
Eucalyptus
Fragrant sumac
Lantana
Pea vine
Red cedar
Red maple
Russian knapweed
Sorghum
Sunflower hulls
Tobacco
Tree of heaven

Gardeners on the Go in the Southwest

Henderen, NV: Ethel M Chocolate Factory & Cactus Garden. Follow up a mouthwatering self-guided tour of this gourmet chocolate factory with a stroll through one of the country's largest cactus collection set in a lush 3-acre garden.

Hatch, NM: Chile Festival. More than 30,000 self-proclaimed "hot heads" descend each Labor Day weekend on this small village to celebrate the annual chile harvest with a parade and the subsequent crowning of the Chile Queen. All manner of chiles—fresh, dried, roasted, and otherwise—are available at various food vendor stalls and exhibits.

Gilroy, CA: Bonefante Gardens, home of the Tree Circus. Grafted into complex, whimsical, and fantastic forms, these amazing trees are the creation of Axel Erlandson, an early twentieth-century farmer with a keen love for the natural world, highly developed grafting skills, and infinite patience for the care and nurturing of his imaginative work. Following Erlandson's death in 1964 the collection languished until, in a legend worthy of fiction, heroic rescue measures were undertaken, culminating in 1985 when twenty-nine trees were moved to their present-day location as the central attraction of this horticultural-based theme park.

Amarillo, TX: Cadillac Ranch. A quintessentially American crop in a rural corner of Texas, a row of Cadillacs (vintage 1949–63) are "planted" nose end down, in a dusty, barren field, painted a lively pink, and covered with layers of graffiti.

Is It Wicker or Rattan?

"Wicker" is the term given to any material that is dried and woven; this can be bamboo, durable grasses, or rattan.

Described as "climbing palms," the Arecaceae family contains thirteen genera and more than 600 different species of plants collectively referred to as "rattan" that have been recognized for use and cultivation. Their major habitat is tropical rain forest, where in much of Southeast Asia they represent the most important forest product after timber. The stems and canes of the plants are harvested as a raw material for furniture and baskets. The fruit of some rattans can drip a red resin called "dragon's blood"; historically this resin was thought to have medicinal properties and was also used as a dye for violins.

Rose Bowl Parade Stats

- *Begun in 1890 and held every New Year's Day in Pasadena, California, unless January 1 falls on a Sunday, pushing the parade to Monday.*
- *Started as a celebration of California's mild winter climate and long growing season.*
- *First parade attended by 3,000 people; today's typical turnout numbers more than a million.*

- *Renowned for its spectacular display of thirty-five to fifty floral floats. Rules dictate that every exposed inch of each float be covered with plant parts, whether fresh, dried, or crushed.*

- *Construction costs run between $100,000 to $300,000 per float, consuming as many flowers as a florist would typically use in 5 years, or about 10,000 pounds.*

- *On average, each float takes more than 7,000 people-hours to decorate.*

Patron Saints of the Garden

Adam
Adelard
Agnes of Rome
Christopher
Dorothy of Caesarea
Fiacre
Gertrude of Nivelles
Phocas the Gardener
Rose of Lima
Sebastian
Thérèse of Lisieux
Tryphon
Urban of Langres

USDA Organic

Instituted on October 21, 2002, the U.S. Department of Agriculture organic standard states the following:

The term, "organic," may only be used on labels and in labeling of raw or processed agricultural products, including ingredients, that have been produced and handled in accordance with the regulations in this part. The term, "organic," may not be used in a product name to modify a nonorganic ingredient in the product . . .

Products sold, labeled, or represented as "100 percent organic." A raw or processed agricultural product sold, labeled, or represented as "100 percent organic" must contain (by weight or fluid volume, excluding water and salt) 100 percent organically produced ingredients . . .

Products sold, labeled, or represented as "organic." A raw or processed agricultural product sold, labeled, or represented as "organic" must contain (by weight or fluid volume, excluding water and salt) not less than 95 percent organically produced raw or processed agricultural products. Any remaining product ingredients must be organically produced, unless not commercially available in organic form, or must be nonagricultural substances or nonorganically produced agricultural products produced consistent with the National List in subpart G of this part [of the standard] . . .

Products sold, labeled, or represented as "made with organic (specified ingredients or food group[s])." Multiingredient agricultural product sold, labeled, or represented as "made with organic (specified ingredients or food group[s])" must contain (by weight or fluid volume, excluding water and salt) at least 70 percent organically produced ingredients, which are produced and handled pursuant to requirements in subpart C of this part [of the standard] . . .

Products with less than 70 percent organically produced ingredients. The organic ingredients in multiingredient agricultural product containing less than 70 percent organically produced ingredients (by weight or fluid volume, excluding water and salt) must be produced and handled pursuant to requirements in subpart C of this part [of the standard]. The nonorganic ingredients may be produced and handled without regard to the requirements of this part. Multiingredient agricultural product containing less than 70 percent organically produced ingredients may represent the organic nature of the product only as provided in §205.305.

Millennium Seed Bank

The Millennium Seed Bank Project is an international collaborative plant conservation initiative. The program was conceived, developed, and is managed by the Royal Botanic Gardens at Kew in England. The worldwide effort aims to safeguard more than 24,000 plant species against extinction, or a goal of at least 10 percent of the world's flora.

The actual seed bank is located in the Wellcome Trust Millennium Building (WTMB), at Wakehurst Place in West Sussex, England. The WTMB opened in 2000 and was touted as the Noah's Ark of plants. As well as storing thousands of seed samples in a large underground vault, the building includes advanced seed research and processing facilities.

In addition to the seed collection, the project endeavors to:

- *Carry out research to improve all aspects of seed conservation*
- *Make seeds available for research and species reintroduction into the wild*
- *Encourage plant conservation throughout the world by facilitating access to and transfer of seed conservation technology*
- *Maintain and promote the public interest in plant conservation*
- *Provide a world-class facility as a focal resource for this activity*

"My advice to the garden clubs of our land is to raise more hell and fewer dahlias."

—ATTRIBUTED TO WILLIAM ALLEN WHITE

(Pulitzer-prize winning writer, best-selling novelist, and prolific freelancer who built the Emporia Gazette of Kansas into one of the nation's finest small-town newspapers from 1895 until his death in 1944)

National Garden Club

Founded in 1929, the National Garden Club is the largest volunteer gardening organization in the world. It has 8,488 chapters and 264,440 members in fifty states and the District of Columbia, with headquarters adjacent to the Missouri Botanical Garden in Saint Louis, Missouri.

Mission statement: National Garden Clubs Inc. provides education, resources, and national networking opportunities for its members to promote the love of gardening, floral design, and civic and environmental responsibility.

Plants "Discovered" by Lewis and Clark

The Rocky Mountains
Yarrow (*Achillea millefolium*)
Geyer's onion (*Allium geyeri*)
Western serviceberry (*Amelanchier alnifolia*)
Piper's anemone (*Anemone piperi*)
Angelica (*Angelica arguta*)
Arrow-leaved balsamroot (*Balsamorhiza sagittata*)
Braided liverwort (*Bazzania trilobata*)
Cat's-ear mariposa lily (*Calochortus elegans*)
Fairy slipper (*Calypso bulbosa*)
Blue camas (*Camassia quamash*)
Long-leaved evening primrose (*Camissonia subacaulis*)
Red-stem ceanothus (*Ceanothus sanguineus*)

Buckbrush ceanothus (*Ceanothus velutinus*)
Green rabbit brush (*Chrysothamnus viscidiflorus*)
Elkhorn (*Clarkia pulchella*)
Western spring beauty (*Claytonia lanceolata*)
Sugarbowl (*Clematis hirsutissima*)
Bunchberry (*Cornus canadensis*)
Shrubby cinquefoil (*Dasiphora fruticosa*)
Silverberry (*Elaeagnus commutata*)
Cut-leaved daisy (*Erigeron compositus*)
Oregon sunshine (*Eriophyllum lanatum*)
Rough wallflower (*Erysimum capitatum*)
Glacier lily (*Erythronium grandiflorum*)
Idaho fescue (*Festuca idahoensis*)
Clustered elkweed (*Frasera fastigiata*)
Yellow bell (*Fritillaria pudica*)
Blanketflower (*Gaillardia aristata*)
Prairie smoke (*Geum triflorum*)
Oceanspray (*Holodiscus discolor*)
Scarlet gilia (*Ipomopsis aggregata*)
Missouri iris (*Iris missouriensis*)
Common juniper (*Juniperus communis*)
Prairie June grass (*Koeleria macrantha*)
Bitterroot (*Lewisia rediviva*)
Three-leaved lewisia (*Lewisia triphylla*)
Fern-leaved desert parsley (*Lomatium dissectum*)
Nine-leaved desert parsley (*Lomatium triternatum*)
Trumpet honeysuckle (*Lonicera ciliosa*)
Bearberry honeysuckle (*Lonicera involucrata*)
Utah honeysuckle (*Lonicera utahensis*)
Silver lupine (*Lupinus argenteus*)
Silky lupine (*Lupinus sericeus*)
Pineapple weed (*Matricaria matricaioides*)

Fool's huckleberry (*Menziesia ferruginea*)
Yellow monkey flower (*Mimulus guttatus*)
Lewis's red monkey flower (*Mimulus lewisii*)
Thin-leaved owlclover (*Orthocarpus tenuifolius*)
Bessey's crazyweed (*Oxytropis besseyi*)
Mountain lover (*Paxistima myrsinites*)
Elephant's-head (*Pedicularis groenlandica*)
Shrubby penstemon (*Penstemon fruticosus*)
Wilcox's penstemon (*Penstemon wilcoxii*)
Virgate phacelia (*Phacelia heterophylla*)
Mock orange (*Philadelphus lewisii*)
Showy phlox (*Phlox speciosa*)
Red mountain heather (*Phyllodoce empetriformis*)
Ponderosa pine (*Pinus ponderosa*)
Sandberg's bluegrass (*Poa secunda*)
Jacob's ladder (*Polemonium pulcherrimum*)
American bistort (*Polygonum bistortoides*)
Black cottonwood (*Popluus trichocarpa*)
Bittercherry (*Prunus emarginata*)
Chokecherry (*Prunus virginiana*)
Bluebunch wheatgrass (*Pseudoroegneria spicata*)
Bitterbrush (*Purshia tridentata*)
Cascara buckthorn (*Rhamnus purshiana*)
Golden currant (*Ribes aureum*)
Sticky currant (*Ribes viscosissimum*)
Narrow-leaved skullcap (*Scutellaria angustifolia*)
Lance-leaved stonecrop (*Sedum lanceolatum*)
Worm-leaved stonecrop (*Sedum stenopetalum*)
Cascade mountain ash (*Sorbus scopulina*)
Snowberry (*Symphoricarpos albus*)
Mountain kittentails (*Synthyris missurica*)
Small-headed clover (*Trifolium microcephalum*)

Purple trillium (*Trillium petiolatum*)
California false hellebore (*Veratrum californicum*)
Bear grass (*Xerophyllum tenax*)
Showy death camas (*Zigadenus elegans*)

The Pacific Forest

Vine maple (*Acer circinatum*)
Big-leaf maple (*Acer macrophyllum*)
Red alder (*Alnus rubra*)
Pacific madrone (*Arbutus menziesii*)
Silverweed (*Argentina anserina*)
Arrow-leaved balsamroot (*Balsamorhiza sagittata*)
Shiny Oregon grape (*Berberis aquifolium*)
Dull Oregon grape (*Berberis nervosa*)
Deer fern (*Blechnum spicant*)
Slender toothwort (*Cardamine nuttallii*)
Edible thistle (*Cirsium edule*)
Miner's lettuce (*Claytonia perfoliata*)
Candy flower (*Claytonia sibirica*)
Cliff larkspur (*Delphinium menziesii*)
Mountain wood fern (*Dryopteris carthusiana*)
Feather boa kelp (*Egregia menziesii*)
Oregon moss (*Eurhynchium oreganum*)
Checker lily (*Fritillaria affinis*)
Salal (*Gaultheria shallon*)
Foxtail barley (*Hordeum jubatum*)
Dune wildrye (*Leymus mollis*)
Gray's desert parsley (*Lomatium grayi*)
Desert parsley (*Lomatium* sp.)
Oregon boxwood (*Paxistima myrsinites*)
Pacific ninebark (*Physocarpus capitatus*)
Douglas fir (*Pseudotsuga menziesii*)

Oregon oak (*Quercus garryana*)
Straggly gooseberry (*Ribes divaricatum*)
Red currant (*Ribes sanguineum*)
Salmonberry (*Rubus spectabilis*)
White trillium (*Trillium ovatum*)
Evergreen huckleberry (*Vaccinium ovatum*)
Red huckleberry (*Vaccinium parvifolium*)

How to Keep Houseplants Watered During an Extended Absence

1. Cut a length of pantyhose about 12 to 18 inches long.
2. Bury one end in the root zone of the soil around the plant.
3. Immerse the other end in a container of water placed above the level of the plant to form a wicking device.

Gardeners on the Go in Hawaii

Wahiawa, HI: The Pineapple Garden Maze at the Dole Plantation. Recognized as the world's largest maze in 2001, this vividly colorful garden planted with hibiscus, pineapple, and other native tropical plants covers more than 2 acres and contains nearly 2 miles of paths.

From Equatorial Africa to Grandma's Kitchen

African violets (*Saintpaulia ionantha*) were introduced to Europe in 1892 by Baron Adalbert Emil Walter Radcliffe le Tanneus von Saint Paul-Illaire, from the then German colony of Tanganyika, today known as Tanzania.

Suggestions for the culture of African violets:

- *Using water at room temperature keep soil moist but never soggy, taking care to not get the leaves of the plant wet, which can cause rot.*

- *Provide bright indirect light (approximately 10,000–12,000 lux or 900–1,100 foot candles if using a light meter) for at least 8 but not more than 16 hours. African violets require 8 hours a day of darkness for flowering to initiate. Turn pot 90 degrees from the light source with each watering to promote a symmetrical growth habit.*

- *Maintain room temperature at about 70°F. Temperatures below 60°F and above 80°F are detrimental to the plant.*

- *Fertilize with a water-soluble African violet food three out of every four waterings.*

Lawn Care 101

Early spring: Clear lawn of debris accumulated over the winter and mow at 2 inches. Address any soil compaction and thinning areas by aerating the soil and overseeding.

Midspring: Maintain lawn at 2½ to 3 inches, mowing as growth rate dictates but at least weekly. Fertilize with a slow-release, preferably organic fertilizer. If desired, a combination product with preemergence weed control should be applied now. *Note:* Most lawn diseases result from overzealous fertilizing in spring.

Summer: Maintain lawn at 3 to 3½ inches to slightly shade the roots and prevent heat or drought stress. Lawns require 1 inch of water a week, either from rainfall or irrigation. Control dandelion and other broadleaf weeds, and monitor for insect activity.

Fall: Gradually lower mowing height back to 2½ inches, continuing to mow weekly. Apply a slow-release fertilizer and treat soil compaction and thinning areas if not attended to in the early spring. Fall is the most effective time to apply herbicides, organic or otherwise, to control broadleaf weeds, as the plants are drawing energy down into their roots, taking the herbicide with it, as they prepare for winter.

Quarantined Plants

Due to the devastating spread of sudden oak death (SOD), caused by the pathogen *Phytophthora ramorum*, interstate transport of the following plants is heavily regulated:

Big-leaf maple (*Acer macrophyllum*)
Bodnant viburnum (*Viburnum* x *bodnantense*)
California bay laurel (*Umbellularia californica*)
California black oak (*Quercus kelloggii*)
California buckeye (*Aesculus californica*)
California coffeeberry (*Rhamnus californica*)
California honeysuckle (*Lonicera hispidula*)
Camellia (*Camellia* spp., all species, hybrids, and
cultivars)
Canyon live oak (*Quercus chrysolepis*)
Coast live oak (*Quercus agrifolia*)
Coast redwood (*Sequoia sempervirens*)
Doublefile viburnum (*Viburnum plicatum*)
Douglas fir (*Pseudotsuga menziesii* var. *menziesii*)
European ash (*Fraxinus excelsior*)
European yew (*Taxus baccata*)
Evergreen huckleberry (*Vaccinium ovatum*)
False Solomon's seal (*Maianthemum racemosum*,
formerly *Smilacina racemosa*)
Himalaya andromeda (*Pieris formosa* and *P. formosa* x
japonica)
Holm oak (*Quercus ilex*)
Laurustinus (*Viburnum tinus*)
Lilac (*Syringa vulgaris*)
Madrone (*Arbutus menziesii*)
Manzanita (*Arctostaphylos manzanita*)
Mountain andromeda (*Pieris floribunda* and *P.
floribunda* x *japonica*)
New Zealand privet (*Griselinia littoralis*)
Persian ironwood (*Parrotia persica*)
Red-tip photinia (*Photinia fraseri*)

Rhododendron (including azalea) (*Rhododendron* spp.,
  all species, hybrids, and cultivars)
Scotch heather (*Calluna vulgaris*)
Shreve's oak (*Quercus parvula* var. *shrevei*)
Southern red oak (*Quercus falcata*)
Sweet chestnut (*Castanea sativa*)
Tan oak (*Lithocarpus densiflorus*)
Toyon (*Heteromeles arbutifolia*)
Western starflower (*Trientalis latifolia*)
Witch hazel (*Hamamelis virginiana*)
Wood rose (*Rosa gymnocarpa*)

The Major Garden Features at Versailles

Le Parterre d'Eau (The Water Parterre)
Le Bassin de Latone (The Fountain of Latona)
L'Allée Royale (The Royal Avenue)
Le Bassin d'Apollon (The Fountain of Apollo)
Le Grand Canal (The Grand Canal)
Le Bassin de Bacchus (The Fountain of Bacchus)
Le Bassin de Saturne (The Fountain of Saturn)
Le Bosquet de la Reine (The Queen's Grove)
Le Bosquet des Rocailles (The Rubble)
Les Quinconces du Midi (The South Quincunxes)
Le Jardin du Roi (The King's Garden)
La Colonnade (The Colonnade)
La Salle des Marronniers (The Chestnut Grove)
Le Bassin de Cérès (The Fountain of Ceres)
Le Bassin de Flore (The Fountain of Flora)
Le Bosquet de L'Encelade (The Encelade)

Le Bosquet des Dômes (The Domes)
Le Bosquet de l'Obélisque (The Obelisk Grove)
Le Bosquet de L'Étoile (The Star Grove)
Le Bosquet du Rond-Vert (The Round Lawn)
Le Bosquet des Bains d'Apollon (The Grove of the
  Baths of Apollo)
La Pièce d'Eau des Suisses (The Pond of the Swiss)
L'Orangerie (The Orangery)
Le Parterre du Midi (The South Parterre)
Le Parterre du Nord (The North Parterre)
La Fontaine de la Pyramide (The Pyramid Fountain)
L'Allée d'Eau (The Water Avenue)
Le Bassin du Dragon (The Dragon Fountain)
Le Bassin de Neptune (The Fountain of Neptune)
L'Arc de Triomphe (The Triumphal Arch)
Les Trois Fontaines (The Three Fountains)

Kir Royale

This elegant mixture of 1 part crème de cassis with 5 parts chilled
champagne is considered the afternoon sip of sophisticates
seated in quaint French sidewalk cafes. In fact, crème de
cassis—a blood-red, sweet, black currant flavored liqueur dating
to the sixteenth century—was first produced by monks as a cure
for snakebites, jaundice, and general wretchedness. Further, the
French slang for Kir is *rince cochon*, a term of endearment that
literally translates as "pig wash."

Holkham Hall Garden Apparatus

Holkham Hall, one of England's grand country houses, was built in Norfolk in the eighteenth century. The park surrounding the estate was designed by Capability Brown (1716–83), a fashionable landscape designer of the day much sought after by landed families. Brown's work was characterized by naturalistic compositions in contrast to the more formal designs of his contemporaries. However, as this 1761 inventory of gardening equipment shows, it takes a lot of work to appear "natural":

20 barrow chairs
3 double-seated chairs
20 small Windsor chairs
6 compass-back chairs
250 pines (pineapples) in pots
4 citrons in tubs
46 orange trees in tubs
9 lemon trees in pots
3 broadleaf myrtles in tubs
25 double- and single-leafed myrtles in pots
70 seedling oranges in pots
13 aloes in pots
11 scythes
6 rakes
4 Dutch hoes
9 English hoes
8 forks
3 jets
6 watering pots
1 house engine, 1 brass hand engine, 2 wooden hand engines
(all for water)

2 tin pipes for watering pines
3 leather pipes
1 suction pipe
1 brass pipe
1 rose (for sprinkling)
2 thermometers
2 shovels
4 hammers
1 hook (sickle)
1 hatchet
2 iron rollers
5 boots for horses to roller the garden with
8 hand baskets for fruit
1 pair of garden shears
1 mallet and pruning chisel
2 mattocks
1 flag shovel
1 edging tool
2 pair of iron reels with lines
2 hand saws
1 grindstone and frame
4 rubstones
1 cucumber cutter
91 frames glazed for melons, pines, and cucumbers
35 frames for the fire walls
21 hand glasses
9 bell glasses, netting in five parcels, and a number of old mats
8 common wheelbarrows
2 water barrows
3 water tubs
3 stone rollers
1 large fruit basket
8 bushel baskets
3 water pails

Gravel Coverage

It takes more than 180 tons of gravel to cover a 1-acre site with a scant 1 inch:

- *43,560 square feet / 324 square feet per cubic yard = 134.44 cubic yards*
- *134.44 cubic yards x 2,700 pounds per cubic yard = 362,988 pounds*
- *362,988 pounds / 2,000 pounds per ton = 181.5 tons*

Hydrangeas: Pink or Blue?

It is widely believed that hydrangeas grown in acidic soil produce blue flowers while the same plants grown in alkaline soil produce pink flowers. While this remains true, science has proven that the key ingredient for flower color variance is aluminum. Acidic soils enable the plant to use the aluminum present in the soil, while alkaline soils cannot convert it into a useable form. Thus, in the absence of aluminum, hydrangea flowers are pink.

Trees

The Oak is called the king of trees,
The Aspen quivers in the breeze,
The Poplar grows up straight and tall,
The Peach tree spreads along the wall,
The Sycamore gives pleasant shade,
The Willow droops in watery glade,
The Fir tree useful timber gives,
The Beech amid the forest lives.

—SARA COLERIDGE (1802–52), ENGLISH POET

American Dahlia Society

The American Dahlia Society lists these flower forms in its
Classification and Handbook of Dahlias:

Anemone-flowered
Collarette
Formal decorative
Incurved cactus
Informal decorative

Laciniated
Mignon single
Miniature ball
Novelty
Novelty fully double
Novelty open
Orchid-flowering
Peony-flowering
Pompom
Semicactus
Single
Stellar
Straight cactus
Water lily

hor·tus de·li·ci·ar·um: Literally a "garden of delights," one of the
many names ascribed to early pleasure gardens whose model was
the Garden of Eden.

Green with Envy

Lust, greed, covetousness, jealousy, and avarice—incontrovertible
if ugly facts of life when dealing with a gardener in the throes of
a particular plant hunger. Empress Josephine, wife of Napoleon
Bonaparte, was devoted to her gardens at Malmaison and was
very protective of her prized plants from all over the world. When

the many plants became too much for her to tend to personally, a gardener was put in charge of the collection, and corruption erupted over that most showy and flamboyant of blooms—the dahlia. One of Josephine's ladies-in-waiting approached the head gardener asking for a tuber, hoping to outdo her mistress's collection. However, the good man refused. Not to be denied, the young lady ordered her lover to bribe the gardener, whereupon 100 roots were promptly produced. When Josephine heard, she was outraged: she dismissed the gardener, her lady-in-waiting, and exiled the lover. She then had all of her dahlias chopped up and never again would hear of the plant in her presence.

A Layer to Spare

Cork as we know it—commonly used to stop a bottle of wine, cover a bulletin board, or provide cushy flooring material—is harvested from the cork oak (*Quercus suber*), the only tree that can survive "bark harvesting" because it has two layers. In recent years winemakers have moved away using actual cork in an effort to conserve the dwindling cork oak population.

Oldest Living Tree

A bristlecone pine (*Pinus aristata*) located in the Wheeler Peak area of Nevada is thought to be 4,900 years old.

Oldest Living Thing on Earth

A creosote bush (*Larrea divaricata*) found in the Mojave Desert is estimated to have grown from a seed nearly 12,000 years ago.

Hedgehogs

Affectionately known as "hedgies," hedgehogs are common in parks, woods, forests, gardens, and farmlands in England and Ireland, where they are protected under the Wildlife and Countryside Act and may not be trapped. The International Hedgehog Association is a nonprofit organization established to educate the public in the care and betterment of hedgehogs and to facilitate the rescue, welfare, promotion, and care of hedgehogs everywhere.

Hedgie Highlights

- *There are fourteen species of hedgehogs.*
- *All hedgehogs are similar in appearance, with sharp, narrow snouts, small eyes, and short legs. They are covered on the back and sides with smooth spines.*
- *The hedgehog is an omnivore, eating both plants and animals. They eat insects, mice, frogs, small birds, worms, caterpillars, slugs, and toads, as well as plants and fruits. Prized in English gardens for slug control, they can also eat small snakes and are especially fond of eggs and will eat them right out of a bird's nest. Less well-known is that hedgehogs are lactose intolerant.*

Lady Bird Johnson's Lasting Legacy

Lady Bird Johnson, born Claudia Alta Taylor, wife of Lyndon B. Johnson, thirty-sixth president of the United States, has always been an environmentalist and a champion of the land. As first lady she worked with then Secretary of the Interior Stewart Udall to establish the First Lady's Committee for a More Beautiful Capital, a privately funded program that oversaw the planting of thousands of woody plants and approximately 2 million flowering bulbs throughout Washington DC in an effort to present a welcoming environment for visitors to the nation's capital. Later, when the program was expanded to include the entire nation, Mrs. Johnson remained in an active role.

Also during her tenure at the White House, Lady Bird Johnson personally lobbied Congress on behalf of the Highway Beautification Act of 1965, the first major legislative campaign launched by a first lady. While largely consisting of laws to control outdoor advertising signage along the country's highways, thanks to her efforts attention was also directed to improving the landscaping along the country's roads.

In 1972, on the occasion of her seventieth birthday, Lady Bird Johnson founded the National Wildflower Research Center, a nonprofit environmental organization dedicated to the preservation and reestablishment of native plants in natural and planned landscapes. In 1997 the center was renamed the Lady Bird Johnson Wildflower Center in honor of Mrs. Johnson's eighty-fifth birthday. Lady Bird Johnson was further honored in 1999 when Secretary of the Interior Bruce Babbitt presented her with the Native Plant Conservation Initiative Lifetime Achievement Award.

Planting Rhyme

Plant your seeds in a row,

One for the pheasant, one for the crow,

One to rot and one to grow.

A Gardener's iPod Playlist

"Honeysuckle Rose," Fats Waller (1929)
"Room Full of Roses," Sons of the Pioneers (1949)
"American Beauty Rose," Frank Sinatra (1950)
"La Vie en Rose," Louis Armstrong (1952)
"Singin' in the Rain," Gene Kelly (1952)
"The Flower Garden of my Heart," Richard Rogers (1952)
"A Blossom Fell," Nat King Cole (1955)
"Cherry Pink and Apple Blossom White," Perez Prado (1955)
"Your Love Is Like a Flower," Lester Flatt (1957)
"The Green Leaves of Summer," Brothers Four (1960)
"Please Don't Eat the Daisies," Doris Day (1960)
"Where Have All the Flowers Gone?," Peter Paul & Mary (1962)

"Roses Are Red (My Love)," Bobbie Vinton (1962)
"Green Green Grass of Home," Tom Jones (1965), Elvis
  Presley (1975)
"Orange Blossom Special," Johnny Cash (1965)
"Safe in My Garden," Mamas & the Papas (1968)
"Tip-Toe Through the Tulips with Me," Tiny Tim (1968)
"The Lemon Song," Led Zeppelin (1969)
"Weren't the Roses Beautiful in May," Nat Stuckey (1969)
"Come to My Garden," Minnie Riperton (1970)
"Rose Garden," Lynn Anderson (1970)
"Dead Flowers," Rolling Stones (1971)
"Good Year for the Roses," George Jones (1971)
"Early Morning Breeze," Dolly Parton (1971)
"Harvest," Neil Young (1972)
"Jungle Boogie," Kool & the Gang (1973)
"Let It Grow," Eric Clapton (1974)
"Jungleland," Bruce Springsteen (1975)
"Jungle Time," Neil Diamond (1976)
"Rose in My Garden," Karla Bonoff (1977)
"Forever Like a Rose," Seals & Crofts (1978)
"Life Is Good in the Greenhouse," XTC (1978)
"Black Orchid," Stevie Wonder (1979)
"Power Flower," Stevie Wonder (1979)
"Secret Life of Plants," Stevie Wonder (1979)
"Venus Fly Trap and the Bug," Stevie Wonder (1979)
"The Rose," Bette Midler (1980)
"Gardening at Night," R.E.M. (1982)
"I'm Looking over a Four Leaf Clover," Jerry Lee Lewis (1984)
"Kiss the Dirt (Falling Down the Mountain)," INXS (1986)
"Flor d'Luna (Moonflower)," Santana (1987)
"Summertime Dream," Gordon Lightfoot (1987)
"Bed of Roses," Screaming Trees (1991)

"Dirt," Alice in Chains (1992)
"Pumpkin Head," Dharma Bums (1993)
"Kiss From a Rose," Seal (1994)
"Sassafrass Roots," Green Day (1994)
"Wildflowers," Tom Petty (1994)
"Secret Garden," Bruce Springsteen (1995)
"Iris," the Goo Goo Dolls (1998)
"Red Dirt Girl," Emmylou Harris (2000)
"In My Garden," the Swans (2003)
"Nature Boy," Nick Cave and the Bad Seeds (2004)

Bach Flower Essences

Bach Flower Essences have been in use all over the world since the 1930s, when they were introduced by Dr. Edward Bach. Dr. Bach, a London-based, well-known medical doctor and homeopath, became disenchanted with traditional medicine's focus on disease rather than the patient, believing emotional imbalances were the root cause of any illness. Influenced by his early work with homeopathy, Dr. Bach turned to plant-based remedies, developing thirty-eight different flower essences. Each essence was identified as corresponding to a specific emotional imbalance, the theory being that balancing a patient's emotional state would free the body to heal itself.

The Original Essences

Agrimony
Aspen
Beech
Centaury
Cerato
Cherry plum
Chestnut bud
Chicory
Clematis
Crabapple
Elm
Gentian
Gorse
Heather
Holly
Honeysuckle
Hornbeam
Impatiens
Larch
Mimulus
Mustard
Oak
Olive
Pine
Red chestnut
Rock rose
Rock water
Scleranthus
Star of Bethlehem
Sweet chestnut
Vervain

Vine
Walnut
Water violet
Wild oat
Wild rose
Willow

Please Don't Eat the Daisies

But by all means enjoy the following edible flowers in salads, vegetable dishes, and sweets and as a colorful garnish to any healthful meal. Never eat flowers that have not been verifiably grown free of chemicals.

Bachelor's button (garnish)
Bee balm dotted mint (float in punch, garnish for salads)
Borage (cucumber taste; garnish, candied, beverages, cold soups)
Chamomile (tea)
Chive blossoms (common or garlic; garnish, salads, soups, flavored oils or vinegars)
Calendula (peppery; colorful salad garnish)
Carnation (cake decoration)
Clary sage (infuse a bitter flavor into tea or wine)
Coreopsis plains dwarf bicolor (decorative in salads)
Daylily (peppery bite to buds and flowers)
Dianthus (spicy clove taste)
English daisy (garnish, salads)
Hibiscus (citrus/cranberry flavor)
Hollyhock (garnish, salads, color for sandwiches)

Lavender (flavored sugar, beverages, desserts, garnish, dried
    stalks as vegetable skewers)
Marigolds, African (*Tagetes erecta* 'Eskimo', 'Giant Sunset';
    strong flavor; garnish)
Marigolds, signet (lemon/tangerine blend; lemony flavor)
Nasturtium (hot and peppery; beautiful spicy addition to
    salads)
Snapdragon (garnish)
Sunflowers (green buds are edible, petals are nice for garnish,
    seeds when mature)
Squash and pumpkin blossoms (stuff and fry blossoms)
Petunias (garnish)
Poppy, Hungarian blue breadseed (seeds)
Rose (flavored vinegars and cream desserts)
Violet (candied, cake decoration, salads)

Croquet Lawn

The playing area of a standard full-sized court (or lawn, both
terms are acceptable) is defined in the laws of the Croquet
Association as a rectangle 35 yards by 28 yards; the ratio of
length to breadth is 5 to 4. These dimensions delineate the
playing area itself measured to the inside edges of the boundary
lines typically marked with chalk, but string may be used.

The ideal surface for a croquet lawn is a level area of even, fine,
and closely mown grass such as that found on a first-class
bowling green. A good firm, fast court is preferable to a soft,
spongy slow one.

Croquet originated in Ireland and gained popularity in England as a pastime of the aristocracy around the mid-nineteenth century. It made its way to the United States and was often played as a less serious version of the English game. While competitive croquet has gained substantial popularity in America, backyard croquet continues to be a source of wholesome family recreation.

Herbal Baths

Herbal baths have long claimed therapeutic benefits, from relieving common aches and pains to alleviating stress and spiritual cleansing. Whatever your goal , there is no dispute as to the pure sensual pleasure of steeping in a warm, fragrant tub scented with fresh or dried herbs.

Fresh herbal bath: Brew a strong tea by pouring 4 cups boiling water over 1¼ cups freshly harvested herbs; cover and steep for 20 minutes. Strain the tea into a tub filled with body-temperature water. Soak for 15–20 minutes to absorb the benefits of the chosen herbs.

Dried herbal bath: Create a tea bag by placing 1¼ cup of dried herbs into a square of muslin; bundle loosely and tie closed with a string, leaving an end long enough to hang the bag from the tub faucet. Fill the tub with body-temperature water and allow the tea bag to steep for several minutes; squeeze bag to release more herbal essence. Soak for 15–20 minutes, as above.

For specific ailments or conditions:

Antifungal . . . . *Basil, thyme, tea tree, lavender*

Bruises, swelling, and pain . . . *Thyme, calendula, comfrey*

Insomnia . . . . *Lemon balm, chamomile, catnip, hops, lavender*

Muscle aches and neuralgia . . *Chamomile, comfrey, thyme, arnica, bay, eucalyptus, rosemary*

Skin rashes and sores . . . . *Comfrey, lemon grass, nettle, chickweed, lavender, sage, rose hip, red clover*

Stimulating . . . . *Parsley, peppermint, ginger, yarrow*

Stress . . . . *Lavender, hops, chamomile, rosemary*

American Daffodil Society

A favorite herald of spring, the daffodil is grown by gardeners of every stripe and disposition. For every cottage garden to wild meadow, formalized bedding to rock garden, there is a daffodil that will not only flourish, but also thrive and multiply. The American Daffodil Society classifies daffodils into the following divisions:

I. *Trumpet daffodils of garden origin*—one flower to a stem; the trumpet is as long as, or longer than, the surrounding petals. The most familiar and widely grown form.

II. *Long-cupped daffodils of garden origin*—one flower to a stem; the cup is more than one-third but less than equal to the length of the surrounding petals. Most daffodils in the trade are of this division.

III. *Short-cupped daffodils of garden origin*—one flower to a stem; the central cup is not more than one-third the length of the surrounding petals. In some forms the cup is so shallow as to be defined as an "eye."

IV. *Double daffodils of garden origin*—distinguished by double flowers; flowers may be one to a stem or present in multiples, depending on the variety.

V. *Triandrus daffodils of garden origin*—flowers are generally smaller and borne in pendant clusters with slightly reflexed petals. Often fragrant.

VI. *Cyclamineus daffodils of garden origin*—one flower to a stem; petals are highly reflexed back from the long slender trumpet. One of the earliest daffodils of the year to bloom.

VII. *Jonquilla daffodils of garden origin*—more than one flower to a stem and most are highly fragrant. Blooms are smaller, yet proportional to the long-cupped form.

VIII. *Tazetta daffodils of garden origin*—the oldest know form of the genus; flowers are borne in clusters on each stem. Suitable for frost-free areas and indoor forcing.

IX. *Poeticus daffodils of garden origin*—one flower to a stem; pure white flattened petals surround a tiny yellow and red "eye." Generally quite fragrant.

X. *Bulbocodium daffodils of garden origin*—one flower to a stem; petals are insignificant and dominated by a prominent central cup, giving rise to the common name "hoop petticoat."

XI. *Split-corona daffodils of garden origin*—one or more flowers to a stem; the central corona or cup is flattened and split by at least one-third of its length, appearing ruffled and butterfly-like.

XII. Miscellaneous daffodils—a division to include all other daffodils of garden origin that do not fit into the other divisions.

XIII. Specie daffodils, including wild forms and wild hybrids—those daffodils distinguished solely by botanical name; flowers are varied and often very small.

Lemon Juice: A Gardener's Aid

Weed killer cocktail: Mix a dash of lemon juice, a generous splash of white vinegar, and 1 ounce of cheap gin in 8 ounces of water. Spray on offending weeds; especially effective on a warm day.

Stop ants in their tracks: Squirt lemon juice around windowsills and doorjambs to repel ants.

Deter pests: Mix a mild soapy solution with a squeeze of lemon juice. Spray on plants to keep pests away.

Relieve mosquito bites: Apply a paste made with lemon juice and cornstarch to bites to take away the itch.

Clean up: Massage hands with a cut lemon after a day in the garden. Any little cut will be excruciating, but nothing cleans dirty nails quicker.

Aaaah *Choo!*

Plants that are wind pollinated and produce large amounts of very fine pollen grains are primarily to blame for seasonal allergies. Some of the worst offenders follow.

Allergenic Trees/Shrubs

Alder (*Alnus*)
Ash (*Fraxinus*)
Bay laurel (*Laurus nobilis*)
Bayberry (*Myrica*)
Birch (*Betula*)
Bottlebrush (*Callistemon*)
Box elder (*Acer negundo*)
California lilac (*Ceanothus*)
Cedar (*Cedrus*)
Cottonwood (*Populus*)
Cypress (*Cupressus*)
Japanese cedar (*Cryptomeria japonica*)
Juniper (*Juniperus*)
Lilac (*Syringa*)
Mulberry (*Morus*)
Oak (*Quercus*)
Olive (*Olea europaea*)
Privet (*Ligustrum*)
Red maple (*Acer rubrum*)
Russian olive (*Eleagnus aungustifolia*)
Silverberry (*Eleagnus pungens*)
Sumac (*Rhus*)
Sweet gum (*Liquidambar*)

Sycamore (*Platanus*)
Walnut (*Juglans*)
Wattle (*Acacia*)
Willow (*Salix*)
Windmill palm (*Trachycarpus*)

Allergenic Flowers/Grasses

Amaranth (*Amaranthus*)
Black-eyed Susan (*Rudbeckia hirta*)
Bunchgrass (*Agrostis*)
Chrysanthemum (*Chrysanthemum*)
Clover (*Trifollium*)
Club moss (*Lycopodium*)
Dahlia (*Dahlia*)
Gardener's-garters (*Phalaris*)
Meadow rue (*Thalictrum*)
Nettle (*Urtica*)
Orach (*Atriplex*)
Orchard grass (*Dactylis*)
Pearl everlasting (*Anaphalis*)
Queen Anne's lace (*Daucus*)
Rye grass (*Lolium*)
Sedge (*Carex*)
Sunflower (*Helianthus*)
Velvet grass (*Holcus*)
Wormwood (*Artemisia*)
Zinnia (*Zinnia*)

Plants with colorful or fragrant flowers pollinated by insects are considered "safe," or nonallergenic, because they produce relatively large, sticky pollen grains in smaller amounts. The following plants are relatively nonallergenic.

Nonallergenic Trees/Shrubs

Aucuba (*Aucuba*)

Australian tea tree (*Leptospermum*)

Barberry (*Berberis*)

Bush anemone (*Carpenteria californica*)

California bay (*Umbellularia californica*)

Camellia (*Camellia*)

Chaste tree (*Vitex agnus-castus*)

Crape myrtle (*Lagerstroemia*)

Dogwood (*Cornus*)

Escallonia (*Escallonia*)

Fern pine (*Podocarpus gracilior*)

Flowering quince (*Chaenomeles*)

Ginkgo (*Ginkgo*)

Heavenly bamboo (*Nandina domestica*)

Hibiscus (*Hibiscus*)

Holly (*Ilex*)

Hydrangea (*Hydrangea*)

Jacaranda (*Jacaranda*)

Loquat (*Eriobotrya*)

Mexican orange (*Choisya ternate*)

Ornamental pear (*Pyrus*)

Rhododendron (*Rhododendron*)

Rock rose (*Cistus*)

Scotch heather (*Calluna*)

Spirea (*Spiraea*)

Strawberry tree (*Arbutus*)

Tulip tree (*Liriodendron tulipifera*)

Western redbud (*Cercis*)

Nonallergenic Flowers

Beardtongue (*Penstemon*)
Bellflower (*Campanula*)
Bleeding heart (*Dicentra*)
Calla lily (*Zantedeschia*)
Columbine (*Aquilegia*)
Daylily (*Hemerocallis*)
Evening primrose (*Oenothera*)
Hollyhock (*Alcea rosea*)
Iris (*Iris*)
Pink (*Dianthus*)
Spiderwort (*Tradescantia*)

American Hemerocallis Society

The American Hemerocallis Society classifies daylilies into the following forms:

Circular......*Appearing round when viewed from the front.*

Double ......*Having more than 6 flower segments.*

Flat.........*Appearing perfectly flat when viewed from the side, except for the concave throat.*

Informal .....*Irregular, widely spaced, or floppy flower segments.*

Polytepalous ..*Having extra whole flower segments on both the outer and inner whorls of the blossom.*

Recurved......*Flared flower segment edges tuck or roll under when viewed from the side.*

Ruffled ......*Having laced, crimped, knobby, or ruffled flower segment edges when viewed from the front.*

Spider . . . . *Flower segments have a length-to-width ratio of 4 to 1 when fully extended.*

Star . . . . *Flower segments are long, pointed, and spaced in a regular manner, appearing starlike when viewed from the front.*

Triangular . . . . *Flower segments form a triangle when viewed from the front.*

Trumpet . . . . . *Overall flower form most closely resembles the funnel form of a true lily when viewed from the side.*

Unusual. . . . . . *This newest registration class includes crispate, quilled, cascading, and spatulate forms.*

Chelsea Garden Show

The venerable Chelsea Garden Show is held each year for 5 days in May. Produced by the Royal Horticultural Society (RHS), the show gardens and the many accompanying exhibits are staged on the grounds of the Royal Hospital Chelsea in downtown London.

First produced in 1862 at the RHS garden in Kensington, the exhibit was then named the Royal Horticultural Society's Great Spring Show. In 1888 when that garden was closed, RHS moved the show to the Temple Gardens, near the Embankment, where it took place each year until 1911. In 1912 the Temple Show was canceled to make way for a one-time horticultural event. Sir Harry Veitch, a well-known nurseryman, secured the grounds of the Chelsea Hospital for the Royal International Horticulture

Exhibit. It proved an excellent location to exhibit, and when the Great Spring Show resumed in 1913 it was held on this site, continuing almost every year since.

The war years presented some interruptions as did the General Strike of 1926, but for the most part the Chelsea Garden Show became the site of not just fabulous show gardens and artful displays, but also fashionable tea parties and visits by the royal family.

Today the Chelsea Garden Show is viewed as one of the most important events in the horticultural calendar, with approximately 157,000 visitors each year—a number limited by the capacity of the venue. Garden designers from around the world as well as avid hobbyists compete for a chance to exhibit, hoping for a coveted award.

Gold, silver-gilt, silver, and bronze awards are presented in the following categories:

Flora . . . . *Gardens and floral exhibits*
Grenfell . *Exhibits of pictures, photographs, floral arrangements, and floristry*
Hogg. . . . *Exhibits of fruit*
Knightian *Exhibits of vegetables, including herbs*
Lindley . . *Exhibits of special educational or scientific interest*

Special honors are awarded for the following:

Best Show Garden
Best Courtyard Garden
Best Chic Garden
Best City Garden

Certificates for Junior displays
RHS Sundries Bowl
RHS Junior Display Trophy
RHS Floral Arrangement Trophies
RHS Floristry Trophies
RHS President's Award
Show certificates of merit

Aphrodisiacs in the Plant World

Aniseed: Popular with ancient Greeks and Romans, who claimed sucking on the seeds would increase desire; a popular dessert flavoring.

Asparagus: Being stoutly phallic in form, this vegetable is said to increase male potency when eaten for 3 straight days.

Avocado: From the Aztec word *ahuacuatl,* literally translated as "testicle tree"; a delicious fruit with a sensuous texture.

Banana: Rich in potassium and B vitamins necessary for sex hormone production, not to mention strongly evocative of the male penis.

Carrots: Reputed to be a male tonic, the phallus-shaped carrot was used by early Middle Eastern royalty to aid seduction.

Cilantro/coriander: A universally embraced "appetite" stimulant.

Figs: Lusciously suggestive of the female sex organs when split open; eat with your fingers.

Garlic: Arouses sexual desire with its inherent heat; less effective, even off-putting, when only one partner partakes of this strongly aromatic herb.

Ginger: Generally stimulates the circulatory system; delicious in many forms.

Horseradish: Popular for renewing strength after sexual exhaustion.

Horsetail: An infusion brewed from fresh stalks stimulates the immune system and prolongs erections.

Licorice root: Said to enhance lust and feelings of love, particularly in women.

Lotus: Long considered a symbol of divine creation with the flower being descriptive of the "cosmic vagina," while the plant as a whole is a symbol of enlightenment, spirituality, and eternal life.

Lovage: Will loosen even the most frigid when drunk as a love potion.

Mustard family: Believed to increase virility, stimulate the sexual glands, and strengthen desire; historically monks were forbidden to ingest mustard seed.

Nutmeg: Promotes a warm contentment in moderation; may produce hallucinogenic effects in large quantities.

Parsley root: Will induce erotic energy.

Pine nuts: Tonic for the libido and rich in zinc, a key mineral for maintaining male potency.

Pineapple: A component in the homeopathic treatment for impotence, rich in vitamin C and quite tasty in rum drinks.

Pomegranate: Long a symbol of fertility and abundance.

Raspberries and strawberries: Described in erotic literature as "fruit nipples," a seductive food to hand-feed your lover.

Rose: Traditional erotic stimulant, especially for women.

Rosemary: Elicits a strong erotic effect when drunk in wine or when applied to the skin by means of a bath.

Sunflower: Fresh petals cooked in oil and served with salt and pepper are said to have a positive power for married couples.

Sweet basil: Invigorates the sex drive, boosts fertility, and said to produce a general sense of well-being for body and mind.

Sweet potato: Contains hormone-like substances stimulating to a woman's sex drive when consumed in quantity.

Yarrow: A useful love potion when steeped in wine or drunk as a tea before intercourse.

Plants Mentioned in the Writings of Colette

Plants of sensual, romantic, and pagan pleasure: Aconite, ageratum, anemone, apple, apricot, azalea, begonia, black pansy, blackberry, caladium, camellia, campanula, canna, carnation, cherry, chimonanthus, chrysanthemum, clematis, corylopsis, crocus, cup-and-saucer vine, currant, daffodil, dahlia, daphne, deutzia, edelweiss, foxglove, gardenia, germander, gloxinia, guilder rose, heliotrope, hellebore, hepatica, herb Robert, hyacinth, hydrangea, impatiens, iris, jasmine, lilac, lily, lily of the valley, lobelia, love-lies-bleeding, lupine, magnolia, mimosa, moonflower, nasturtium, nicotiana, nigella, orange, orchid, pampas grass, peach, pear, peony, pineapple, pittosporum, plum, poppy, potentilla, primrose, quill, quince, raspberry, rose, saffron crocus, snowdrop, Solomon's seal, sumac, tansy, thrift, tuberose, tulip, veronica, violet, wallflower, walnut, weigelia, wild strawberry, wisteria, wood anemone, zinnia.

Natural Air Conditioners

While all plants take in carbon dioxide and emit oxygen, the following are especially effective at filtering air pollution and cleaning up toxins common in office buildings, homes, and other closed environments:

>   Areca palm
>   Arrowhead vine
>   Boston fern
>   Chrysanthemum
>   Date palm
>   Dracena
>   English ivy
>   Peace lily
>   Pothos
>   Rubber tree
>   Spider plant
>   Weeping fig

Bonsai Terminology

chokkan	*formal upright*
moyogi	*informal upright*
shakan	*slanting*
fukinagashi	*windswept*
sabamiki	*split-trunk*
sharimiki	*driftwood*
tanuki	*"cheats"; where sapling is attached to deadwood; also known as a "pheonix graft"*
hokidachi	*semicircular dome or broom*
kengai	*cascade*
han kengai	*semicascade*
shidare-zukuri	*weeping*
bunjin	*single, slender trunk*
negari	*exposed root*
sekjoju	*root over rock*
ishi seki	*planted on rock*
sokan	*twin-trunk*
sankan	*triple-trunk*
kabudachi	*multiple-trunk or clump form*
netsunagari	*root-connected*
yose ue	*group planting*
sai-kei	*landscape planting*
pen-jing	*landscape planting*
shari	*deadwood on trunk*
jin	*deadwood branch*
nebari	*trunk-base/surface roots*
yamadori	*collected material*
suiban	*shallow water tray to display rock plantings*
tokonoma	*traditional Japanese display area*
bonkei	*tray landscape containing rocks and small accent plants as well as trees*

Insects Controlled by Bt

Bacillus thuringiensis, commonly referred to as Bt, is an insecticidal bacterium first isolated in 1911 and named after its place of discovery, Thuringia, Germany.

> **Kurstaki Strain** (for control of leaf-eating caterpillars)
> Alfalfa caterpillar
> Alfalfa webworm
> Cabbage looper
> Cabbageworm (imported)
> Diamondback moth
> European corn borer
> Fall webworm
> Leaf-roller
> Pine budworm
> Pine butterfly
> Red-humped caterpillar
> Sphinx moth
> Spiny elm caterpillar
> Tent caterpillar
> Tomato and tobacco hornworm
> Western spruce budworm
>
> **Israelensis Strains** (for control of fly larvae)
> Black fly
> Fungus gnat
> Mosquito

San Diego/Tenebrionis Strain (for control of leaf beetles)
Colorado potato beetle
Cottonwood leaf beetle
Elm leaf beetle

Bulbous Corm, Tuber, or Just a Fleshy Root?

True bulbs contain all five of the following structures:

Basal plate. . . . . *Area at the base of the bulb from which the roots grow*
Fleshy scales . . . . . . *Primary storage tissue*
Tunic. . . . . *Skinlike covering to protect fleshy scales*
Shoot . . . . *Developing flower and leaf buds*
Lateral buds . . . . . . *Future bulblets or offsets*

Examples: Tulips, daffodils, hyacinths, and lilies. (Lilies are imbricate; that is, absent the tunic or papery covering to protect the fleshy scales.)

Corms are a swollen stem base that is modified into a mass of storage tissue. Corms are distinguished from true bulbs in that they do not contain a developing shoot. Examples: Crocus, gladiolus, and montbretia.

Tubers differ from bulbs and corms in that they do not have a basal plate or a protective tunic covering. Examples: Caladium, anemone, begonia, and the common potato.

Tuberous roots differ from other root structures in that nutrient stores are held in the swollen fingerlike roots of a plant rather than in an enlarged stem or other bulblike structure. Example: Dahlia.

Rhizomes are storage structures that grow horizontally just beneath the surface of the soil. In some cases these can be extremely invasive. Examples: Bearded iris, lily of the valley, and bamboo.

Fleshy-rooted perennials have developed thickened root systems that serve as nutrient stores. Examples: Daylily and peony.

The Garden According to Dewey Decimal

570 Life sciences
576 Microbiology
577 General nature of life
580 Botanical sciences
581 Botany
582 Spermatophyta (seed-bearing plants)
583 Dicotyledones
584 Monocotyledones
585 Gymnospermae (pinophyta)
586 Cryptogamia (seedless plants)
587 Pteridophyta (vascular cryptograms)
630 Agriculture
631 Techniques, equipment, materials
632 Plant injuries, diseases, pests
633 Field and plantation crops
634 Orchards, fruits, forestry
635 Garden crops (horticulture)
710 Civic and landscape art
712 Landscape architecture
713 Landscape architecture of trafficways
714 Water features

El Niño

El Niño refers to a climatic pattern that begins with a massive warming of equatorial South American coastal waters in the Pacific Ocean, generally around Christmas time (El Niño, Spanish for "the little boy," refers to the Christ child). The impact on weather throughout the world during such periods is profound. In North America El Niño winters are typically warmer than normal in the upper Midwest and Canada, while California, northwest Mexico, and the Southeast experience increased rainfall and flooding. By contrast the Pacific Northwest tends to be both drier and warmer. The ramifications on snow pack, water resources, agriculture, and the horticultural industry are widespread and often negative.

It is not uncommon for an El Niño weather pattern to be followed by a La Niña pattern, where climate fluctuations and effects are typically the opposite of those produced by El Niño: increased rainfall followed by drought, mild winters followed by abnormally harsh conditions, and areas of drought experience excessive rainfall—a righting of the climatic balance, so to speak, but one that brings still more weather-related implications for those affected.

A Year of American Arbor Days

Month	Days	State(s)
January	3rd Friday	Florida, Louisiana, Texas
	1st Friday following Feb. 1	Arizona
	2nd Friday	Mississippi
February	1st Friday after the 2nd Monday	Oklahoma
	3rd Friday	Georgia
	Last full week	Alabama
	Feb. 28	Nevada
	1st Friday	Tennessee
	Mar. 7–14	California
March	2nd Friday	New Mexico
	1st Friday following Mar. 15	North Carolina
	3rd Monday	Arkansas
	Last Friday	Kansas
	1st Wednesday	Maryland
	1st Friday	Kentucky
	1st Friday after the 1st Tuesday	Missouri
	2nd Wednesday	Washington
	2nd Friday	Indiana, Virginia, West Virginia
	3rd week	Michigan
	Apr. 22	Nebraska
April	3rd Friday	Colorado
	Last Monday	Wyoming
	Last Friday	Delaware, District of Columbia, Idaho, Illinois, Iowa, Minnesota, Montana, New Hampshire, New Jersey, New York, Ohio, Oregon, Pennsylvania, Rhode Island, South Dakota, Utah, Wisconsin
	Apr. 30	Connecticut, Massachusetts
	1st Friday	North Dakota, Vermont
May	3rd Monday	Alaska
	3rd Week	Maine
November	1st Friday	Hawaii
December	1st Friday	South Carolina

Companion Planting: Creating Wholesome Friendships in the Garden

It has long been recognized that some plants benefit from the presence of specific plants growing nearby, while other pairings have proved contentious (although less is known about the hows or whys of plant antagonisms). A companion planting may function effectively in several ways:

- *Plants with an especially strong fragrance can deter pests by confusing insects who generally navigate by their sense of smell. Herbs, marigolds, and members of the onion family are valuable in this manner.*

- *Plants effective in attracting insects can trap pests, luring them away from the main crop, while in other cases beneficial insects that dine on other garden pests are attracted.*

- *Quick-growing plants can make efficient use of the area between slower to mature plants, reaching harvesting size before their neighbors need the space. Some shallow-rooted plants can be grown alongside more deeply rooted plants, where they will not compete for water and nutrients. In both cases the gardener is effectively producing two crops in the space of one.*

Companion Plants

Common Vegetable	Friends	Rivals
Beans	Beets, broccoli, cabbage, carrots, cauliflower, celery, corn, cucumbers, eggplants, peas, potatoes, radishes, squash, strawberries, tomatoes	Garlic, onion, peppers, sunflowers
Cabbage	Beans, celery, cucumbers, dill, kale, lettuce, onions, potatoes, rosemary, sage, spinach, thyme	Broccoli, cauliflower strawberries, tomatoes
Carrots	Beans, lettuce, onions, peas, radishes, rosemary, sage, tomatoes	Anise, dill, parsley
Corn	Beans, cucumbers, lettuce, melons, peas, potatoes, squash, sunflowers	Tomatoes
Cucumber	Beans, cabbage, cauliflower, corn, lettuce, peas, radishes, sunflowers	Aromatic herbs, melons, potatoes
Lettuce	Asparagus, beets, Brussels sprouts, cabbage, carrots, corn, cucumbers, eggplants, onions, peas, potatoes, radishes, spinach, strawberries, sunflowers, tomatoes	Broccoli
Onion/garlic family	Beets, broccoli, cabbage, carrots, lettuce, peppers, potatoes, spinach, tomatoes	Beans, peas, sage
Peppers	Basil, coriander, onions, spinach, tomatoes	Beans, kohlrabi
Radishes	Beans, carrots, cucumbers, lettuce, tomatoes	Hyssop
Tomatoes	Asparagus, basil, beans, borage, carrots, celery, dill, lettuce, melons, onions, parsley, peppers, radishes, spinach, thyme	Broccoli, Brussels sprouts, cabbage, cauliflower, corn kale, potatoes

Food Fight

Diet has been shown to play an important role in as many as 35 percent of all cancer deaths. The American Cancer Society recommends the following foods for their ability to fight cancer as well as for their healthful benefits:

Apples
Apricots
Bok choy
Broccoli
Brussels sprouts
Cabbage
Cantaloupe
Carrots
Cauliflower
Chickpeas
Collards
Dried beans and corn
Eggplant
Garlic
Ginger
Grapefruit
Kale
Oranges
Parsley
Peaches
Pears
Peppers (red and green)
Potatoes
Prunes

Raspberries
Raisins
Spinach
Strawberries
Sweet potatoes
Tomatoes
Watermelon
Whole grains
Winter squash

Banana/Rose Connection

Bury banana skins beneath roses to add valuable phosphates,
calcium, sulfur, silica, sodium, and magnesium—all marvelous
soil conditioners. People have also been known to bury fish heads
and placentas to aid in plant growth.

Founding Principles of Permaculture

"Permaculture"—an aggregate of the words "permanent" and
"agriculture"—was coined by Australians Bill Mollison and David
Holmgren in the 1970s to describe a productive and sustainable
method of food production, land use, and community building
integrating principles of ecology, landscape design, organic
practices, architecture, and forestry. All permaculture principles
embody the following three core values or ethics:

- *Earthcare:* Respect for the Earth as the source of and support for all life.

- *Peoplecare:* Support and assist one another to develop ways of living that do not harm the planet or each other.

- *Fairshare:* Ensure that the Earth's limited resources are used in a manner that is equitable and fair by placing limitations on consumption.

Urban Agriculture

In the United Kingdom an "allotment" is a small area of land let out for a nominal annual fee by the local government or allotment managing authority for individuals to cultivate and garden, a practice that began in the eighteenth century.

The 1970s saw the birth of a similar concept in Seattle, Washington, called the P-Patch garden program. When the Picardo family truck farm ceased being profitable, the family allowed a local activist, Darlyn Rundberg Del Boca, to use the land to teach children about gardening, donating the produce to Neighbors in Need for the city's hungry. Parents who brought their children to participate in the program were offered areas to "grow their own" and a vital community garden tradition was born.

While the "P" in P-Patch is to honor the contribution of the Picardo family, informally it also stands for People Producing Peas in Public. Similar P-Patch garden programs have since sprung up throughout the country, providing good food, fresh air, and educational opportunities for their many participants.

Corpse Flower

Amorphophallus titanium produces the world's largest unbranched flower, with individual blooms attaining nearly 9 feet in height. Commonly know as the Titan Arum, or corpse flower, the plant is a native of the Sumatran rain forest. Each bloom consists of an enormous phallic shaped spadix wrapped by a spathe appearing to be a single petal. While the bloom only lasts for a few days, its strong fragrance (stench?) of rotting meat attracts the carrion-eating beetles and "flesh flies" that pollinate the beast.

Wears the Love

What is now considered the symbol of love was once a recognized sign of disgrace. A rose, the emblem of Venus, the Greek goddess of love, was once worn by prostitutes to advertise their "wares."

A Time to Sow

An old wives' tale says "never sow seeds when the moon is waning." Because even the tiniest bit of water is influenced by the lunar effect on the Earth's magnetic field, this in fact proves true. Look for a good rain following a new moon—an excellent time to plant your seeds.

---

her·bar·i·um: An assortment of plants that have been dried, pressed and arranged, generally in album form, in some way that makes sense to the plant collector. Sample criteria may be by geographical region, alphabetical by genus, or simply those plants collected over the course of a single summer. Specimens are to be accurately labeled by plant name, date, and location collected, documenting the plants chosen but also providing a reference for future research and education. The herbarium at the Royal Botanic Gardens in Kew, England, contains more than 7 million specimens, representing nearly 98 percent of all the genera in the world. On a more modest scale, the "Science Scrapbook on Flowers," a secondary-school project of Lorraine Ringenbach, circa 1940, contains 14 specimens.

Garden for the Homesick Bride

To cheer his homesick bride, Nebuchadnezzar II built the fabled
Hanging Gardens of Babylon around 600 BC. Amytis, who
hailed from the lush mountainous regions of Medes, found the
arid sun-baked plains of Babylon (present-day Iraq) depressing.
In an effort to re-create her homeland, the king built an artificial
mountain with rooftop gardens. The resulting elaborate series
of towers and terraces planted with large trees, vines, and other
verdant vegetation were extensively documented by early Greek
historians and are considered one of the Seven Wonders of the
World, even though little physical evidence of their existence has
ever been uncovered.

Thorn Removal

Splinters and thorns are an undeniable reality in the cultivation
of a garden, and sooner or later one will lodge in a finger. Left
unattended, the area will become inflamed, tender, and subject to
infection. To quickly remove the offending culprit, firmly press
the edge of a teaspoon to the end of the splinter that is deepest
in the skin. The resulting pressure will force it to the surface,
where you can safely extract it with the flick of a sterile needle.

How to Candy a Violet

Candied violets are an old-fashioned decoration for cakes and other sweet desserts. Present-day commercially produced products resemble lurid blobs that taste strongly of cheap perfume. Fortunately, home preparation of these delicacies is easily within the ability of the discerning gardener/cook.

1. Pick a quantity of sweet violets early in the day when they are fresh from the morning dew. Remove the leaves but keep a long stem on each blossom to assist in handling.
2. Thoroughly wash the blooms clean of any garden soil or dust and carefully blot dry.
3. With a fine paintbrush, holding an individual flower by its stem, paint a mixture of lightly whipped egg white thinned with a little water on each petal, taking care to completely coat both top and bottom.
4. Dip the now-coated blossom gently into a bowl of finely granulated sugar, spooning the sugar to completely cover every part of the flower.
5. Lay the resulting candied violet on a tea towel to dry completely.
6. Snip off the remaining stem before using the violet to adorn your dessert.

Violets may be candied when blooms are plentiful and—once completely dried—stored in a clean, airtight container for use later in the year when they will bring a breath of fresh spring to any sweet dessert.

'Mortgage Lifter' Tomatoes

In the 1930s M. C. Byles of Logan, West Virginia, began crossing and selecting tomato plants in an effort to produce a stable variety that would yield enormous fruit. Byles named the final result of this backyard trial 'Mortgage Lifter' because he sold starts of his plant for a dollar apiece and paid off his six-thousand-dollar mortgage in only 6 years. 'Mortgage Lifter' bears large, pink-fruited beefsteak tomatoes with a mild flavor. Not particularly juicy or in any way a knockout, the 'Mortgage Lifter' is simply reliable and stolid like its resourceful developer.

Recommended Strawberry Varieties by Region

Pacific Northwest

'Benton' *Short-day; bountiful crop of large delicious berries produced in early summer.*

'Rainier' *Short-day; beautiful tasty berries, crop in midsummer.*

'Tristar' *Day-neutral; reliable production of flavorful fruit all summer.*

California

'Albion' *Day-neutral; productive heat-tolerant plants produce delicious large berries over a long season.*

'Fern' *Day-neutral; tasty, medium-sized dark red fruit.*

'Tioga' *Short-day; large flavorful fruit and high yields.*

Southwest

'Guardian' *Short-day; productive yield of berries with excellent flavor.*

'Ozark Beauty' *Day-neutral; delicious bright red fruit.*

'Tioga' *Short-day; good-sized crimson berries with a rich flavor.*

Midwest

'Erliglow' *Short-day; modest early crop of exceptionally flavorful fruit.*

'Jewel' *Day-neutral; flavorful berries, first crop late in the summer with a smaller second crop in early fall.*

'Winona' *Short-day; late crop of large, firm flavorful berries.*

Southeast

'Eariglow' *As above (see Midwest).*

'Benton' *As above (see Pacific Northwest).*

'Titan' *Day-neutral; consistent harvest of beautiful, delicious fruit.*

Northeast

'Cavendish' *Short-day; early season crop of high-quality, flavorful fruit.*

'Elsanta' *Day-neutral; temperamental plants requiring careful cultivation and yielding large quantities of fragrant, tasty fruit.*

'Erliglow' *As above (see Midwest).*

A Rose Is a Rose Is a Rose . . . or Is It?

None of the following plants with common names containing "rose" are in any way related to a true rose:

Christmas or Lenten rose	*Winter-blooming perennial with flowers that resemble five-petaled roses.*
Desert rose	*Small succulent shrub with showy flowers, often grown indoors.*
Moss rose	*The popular low-growing annual, portulaca.*
Mountain rose	*Tendril-climbing vine that produces bright pink flowers.*
Rock rose	*A genus of shrubs with showy flowers that resemble single roses.*
Rose acacia	*Attractive shrub with showy pink flowers in May and June.*
Rose apple	*Tropical tree grown for its fruit.*
Rose campion	*Silver-foliaged weedy perennial more commonly known as "dusty miller."*
Rose mallow	*Common name for members of the showy-flowered Hibiscus genus.*
Rose of Heaven	*Annual that produces flowers of various colors.*
Rose of Jericho	*Small annual herb, also called "resurrection plant" because the mature plant rolls up into a dry ball that uncurls when moistened.*
Rose of Sharon	*An upright, summer-flowering hardy shrub, also called "rose of China" and "Chinese rose."*
Rose root	*Fragrant-rooted succulent perennial.*

Vines

"Quite the Ampelopsis isn't he?"

—LORD PETER WHIMSEY IN *Busman's Honeymoon*,
BY DOROTHY L. SAYERS (1937)

Botanically speaking, vines have developed a range of methods for climbing not to adorn a romantic arbor but to assist the plant in reaching the sun in crowded, competitive native environments. A vine with rootlets or small sucker pads along its length can adhere to a vertical surface. Vines that produce winding tendrils can grasp stems and other narrow structures, while twining vines wrap themselves entirely around their support.

Rootlet Vines

Boston ivy (*Parthenocissus tricuspidata*)
Climbing hydrangea (*Hydrangea anomala* ssp.
 petiolaris)
Ivy (*Hedera*)
Silver-vein creeper (*Parthenocissus henryana*)
Trumpet vine (*Campsis*)
Wintercreeper (*Euonymus fortunei*)

Tendril Vines

Chilean glory-flower (*Eccremocarpus*)
Grape (*Vitis*)
Passionflower (*Passiflora*)
Porcelain berry vine (*Ampelopsis*)

Twining Vines

Bittersweet (*Celastrus*)
Chilean jasmine (*Mandevilla*)
Chocolate vine (*Akebia*)
Dutchman's-pipe (*Aristolochia*)
Honeysuckle (*Lonicera*)
Kiwi (*Actinidia*)
Magnolia vine (*Schisandra*)
Silver-lace vine (*Polygonum*)
Wisteria (*Wisteria*)

The Garden's Gentle Lore

Planting

❧ *The most fruitful time to plant is on days ruled by Scorpio, Pisces, Taurus, or Cancer.*

❧ *Sow peas and beans in the wane of the moon; who soweth them sooner, soweth too soon.*

❧ *Sow fennel, sow trouble.*

❧ *Plant catnip and the cats will get it, sow it and the cats won't know it.*

❧ *Planting rue in your garden will deter Japanese beetles.*

Foretelling the Harvest

❧ *Much snow, much hay.*

❧ *A mild winter and cold summer mean a poor harvest.*

❧ *If it rains on June 8, a wet harvest will follow.*

❧ *No sun, no showers, no summer flowers.*

❧ *When ladybugs arrive, expect a good crop.*

❧ *Early insects, early spring, good crops.*

Corn Lore

❧ *A late spring is favorable to corn but not cattle.*

❧ *Thunder in March, corn to parch.*

❧ *Sow corn when oak leaves are the size of a mouse's ear.*

❧ *Corn planted in Leo will have small ears.*

❧ *In planting corn, four kernels to a hill: one for the blackbird, one for the crow, one for the cutworm, and one to grow.*

❧ *More corn grows in crooked rows.*

❧ *Corn should be knee-high by the Fourth of July.*

❧ *Don't shuck your corn till the cows come home.*

❧ *A full ear of corn will bend its head; an empty ear will stand upright.*

❧ *An armful of weeds is worth an ear of corn.*

A Shade-Dappled Garden for
Disaster Preparedness

In an area of the garden with good moisture-retentive soil in
partial to full shade, place a clump of three white hellebores
(*Helleborus orientalis*). Back this planting with a single mature
clump of black cohosh (*Actaea racemosa*, formerly called
Cimicifuga racemosa). Site a maidenhair fern (*Adiantum pedatum*)
to one side, where it will receive more shade than not, and place
a stand of horse mint (*Monarda punctata*) on the other more
sunny side. Underplant all with a carpet of American pennyroyal
(*Mentha pulegium*).

This quiet composition of green foliage and refreshing white
blooms will not only offer blooming interest over many months,
but you will be well prepared for the following calamities should
they arise:

Colicky infant *An infusion of American pennyroyal is helpful.*
Nasty cold *Drink a strong infusion of horse mint to sweat a*
  fever.
Open wound *Apply white hellebore to the affected area.*
Poisoning *Ingest maidenhair fern to induce vomiting.*
Snakebite *Black cohosh is an antidote.*

Noxious Weeds

Legally, a noxious weed is a nonnative plant that once established is highly destructive, competitive, or difficult to control. Designation is determined on a federal, state, or county basis, reflecting the varying impact of each plant within a specific environment; for instance, a plant that may prove threatening to a wetland environment may not pose a risk in the absence of wetlands. Noxious weeds pose an ecological and economic threat to agricultural land, disrupt native and beneficial plant communities, endanger both animal and human public health, and destroy recreational and private property.

National Invasive Weeds Awareness Week

Annually, in late February, representatives from weed-management agencies and concerned citizens throughout the country gather in an effort to shed light on the increasingly difficult problem of invasive weeds and to brainstorm government as well as grassroots solutions.

Can Plants Tell Time?

The renowned eighteenth-century botanist, Carl Linnaeus, father of taxonomy, was obsessed with the idea of a flower clock, or "watch of Flora" as he referred to it. He compiled a list of forty-six flowers that opened and closed at predictable times throughout a 24-hour period. The resulting garden—believed to be conceptual rather than a reality due to the climatic limitation of his northern European garden in Hammersby, Sweden—contained plants from throughout the world.

Following Linnaeus's lead, in the nineteenth century it became popular for gardeners to plant up actual clock gardens. Circular flowerbeds were laid out in twelve segments to represent the face of a clock, with each segment containing flowers that opened at the time represented by its placement within the garden. Such a garden might contain:

5 A.M.	*Morning glory vine*
6 A.M.	*Daylily and catmint*
7 A.M.	*Dandelion*
8 A.M.	*African daisy, scarlet pimpernel, and red catchfly*
9 A.M.	*Gentian, marigold, ice plant, chickweed, and moss rose*
10 A.M.	*California poppy*
11 A.M.	*Star of Bethlehem and sweet peas*
Noon	*Passionflower*
1–3 P.M.	*In the heat of the day the garden pauses; place a bench to signify repose.*

4 P.M.	*Four-o'clocks*
5 P.M.	*Evening primrose*
6 P.M.	*Moonflower, flowering tobacco, and angel's-trumpet*

Fairy Rings

Occasionally during the spring and summer months, perfect rings of dark green or brown will suddenly and mysteriously appear in areas of turf. These circles can range from a few inches to 50 feet in diameter and at one time were believed to signify areas where fairies had danced during the previous night. In fact, such spectacles are the result of a fungus. Field mushrooms grow and release their spores in a circle just outside the diameter of their cap. These spores establish and exhaust the soil of its nutrients, moving outward in a circular pattern with each subsequent generation of growth. Circular brown patches indicate areas of soil depletion, while deep green circles of growth result from the nitrogen released by the breakdown of organic matter in the soil by the fungi.

Fend Off Barking Dogs

Friend or foe, a barking dog can be alarming. Carry the leaves of the hound's-tongue plant (*Cynoglossum officinale*) and when confronted by a slathering beast put them under your feet and stand your ground to quiet the dog.

What's Your Sign?

Nicholas Culpeper (1616–54), a well-known English physician and herbalist, originated the notion of the stars' astrological influence on disease and the use of associated "vulgar and common herbs" in the treatment of said disease.

Astrological Influences on the Body		
Sign	**Areas of Body**	**Herb**
Aries	Rules conditions of the head and the organs contained within it	Mustard, garlic, onions, nettles, radishes, poppies, peppers, rhubarb, blackberry, marjoram.
Taurus	Rules the neck, throat, ears, mouth, brain stem, and the seven cervical vertebrae	Daisy, dandelion, myrtle, gourds, flax, lilies, larkspur, spinach, moss, lovage.
Gemini	Rules the upper body, including the shoulders, arms, lungs, and breath	Madder, tansy, vervain, woodbine, yarrow, meadowsweet, privet, dog grass.
Cancer	Rules the breasts, esophagus, diaphragm, liver, and stomach	Daisy, alder, lemon balm, rushes, cucumbers, squashes, melons, honeysuckle, hyssop, jasmine.
Leo	Rules the spine, back, and heart	Angelica, bay laurel, borage, chamomile, fennel, dill, saffron, mint, lavender, parsley.
Virgo	Rules the abdominal region, liver, spleen, and intestines	Barley, oats, rye, wheat, skullcap, woodbine, valerian, millet, endive, privet.
Libra	Rules the lumbar regions, kidneys, reproductive fluids, skin, adrenals, and internal reproductive organs	White rose, strawberry, violet, watercress, primrose, pansy, heartsease, lemon thyme.
Scorpio	Rules the nose, kidneys, sacral vertebrae, blood, genitals, bladder, rectum, prostate, uterus, and external reproductive organs	Basil, heather, horehound, bramble, bean, leek, wormwood, blackthorn.
Sagittarius	Rules the lower back, hips, thighs, and sciatic nerve	Mallow, wood betony, feverfew, agrimony.
Capricorn	Rules the knees, skin, hair, and joints	Comfrey, henbane, nightshade, black poppy.
Aquarius	Rules the legs below the knees and the ankles	Myrrh, frankincense, spikenard.
Pisces	Rules the feet and toes	Mosses that grow in the water, ferns, seaweed.

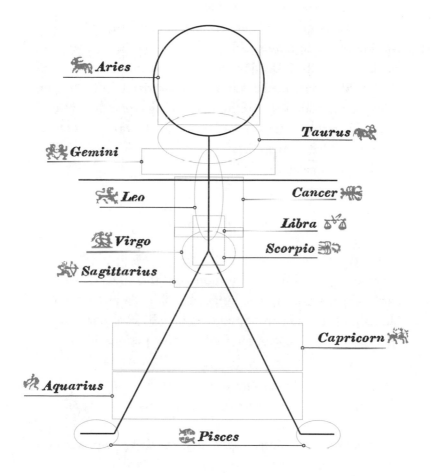

Aries

Taurus

Gemini

Leo

Cancer

Libra

Virgo

Scorpio

Sagittarius

Capricorn

Aquarius

Pisces

Corn Smut: Field Blight or Culinary Delicacy?

Corn smut, or *huitalcoche* in polite company, is a mushroomlike fungus that grows on ears of corn. American farmers have long considered the condition a blight for its negative effect on overall yield, and have typically destroyed infected crops. But in Mexico *huitalcoche* is considered a delicacy and is prized for its pungent, smoky flavor and earthy aroma, demanding a premium price far greater than that of the original corn crop. It was not until the 1990s that adventurous chefs introduced the "Mexican truffle" to the American palate.

Average Seed Life

Most seed packets contain far more seed than the average gardener sowing a city-sized vegetable plot can make use of. Under proper storage conditions—generally cool, dark, and dry— leftover seed can be kept for the following periods of time:

1 year	*Onion, sweet corn*
2 years	*Pepper, beet, okra*
3 years	*Bean, broccoli, carrot, cucumber, lettuce, pea, spinach, tomato*
4 years	*Cabbage, cauliflower, chard, eggplant, kale, mustard, pumpkin, squash, turnip*
5 years	*Collards, cress, muskmelon, radish, watermelon*

Minty Fresh Vases

To ensure freshness and a long life for cut flower bouquets, vases must be kept scrupulously free of dirt and bacteria. Here's a trick for awkward shapes and narrow-neck bottles, which can prove difficult to clean. Fill vase with lukewarm water and add 1–2 denture-cleaning tablets, depending on the volume of the container. Allow to stand overnight for sparkling clean vessels free of mineral deposits and dried-on scum.

Flower Paintings by Georgia O'Keefe

"A flower touches almost everyone's heart."

—GEORGIA O'KEEFE (1887–1996), AMERICAN PAINTER

Black Iris, 1926, oil on canvas, 36" x 30" (*Iris chrysographes*)

Red Poppy, 1927, oil on canvas, 7" x 9" (*Papaver orientale*)

Two Calla Lilies on Pink, 1928, oil on canvas, 40" x 30" (*Zantedeschia aethiopica*)

Series of black-flowered jack-in-the-pulpits (*Arisaema triphyllum*), showing the increasing abstraction of O'Keefe's subject matter: *Jack-in-the-Pulpit II*, 1930, oil on canvas, 40" x 30"; *Jack-in-the-Pulpit III*, 1930, oil on canvas, 40" x 30"; *Jack-in-the-Pulpit IV*, 1930, oil on canvas, 40" x 30"; *Jack-in-the-Pulpit V*,

1930, oil on canvas, 48" x 30"; *Jack-in-the-Pulpit VI*, 1930, oil on canvas, 36" x 18"

Black Hollyhock, Blue Larkspur, 1930, oil on canvas, 30" x 40" (*Alcea rosea, Delphinium consolida*)

Bleeding Heart, 1932, pastel, 15" x 10" (*Dicentra spectablis*)

The White Trumpet Flower, 1932, oil on canvas, 30" x 40" (*Datura suavolens*)

Sunflower for Maggie (Sunflower, New Mexico I), 1935, oil on canvas, 20" x 16" (*Helianthus annus*)

Two Jimson Weeds, 1938, oil on canvas, 36" x 30" (*Datura stamonium*)

An Orchid, 1941, Pastel 27" x 21" (*Cattelya* orchid)

Mother's Day

Mother's Day is the high holiday of the nursery trade, and while it has long been considered a tradition to buy Mom a hanging fuchsia basket, it can be difficult to choose from the many varieties available. All are various color combinations of pink, white, coral, red, purple, and magenta; some are double, some are single, some are tiny, and some are enormous.

'Amelie Aubin', 'Annabel', 'Baby Blue Eyes', 'Balkon', 'Beacon Rosa', 'Ben Jammin', 'Bicentennial', 'Blue Satin', 'Brutus', 'Candy Bells', 'Cara Mia', 'Carla Johnston', 'Celia Smedley', 'Checkerboard', 'Chillerton Beauty', 'Cliantha', 'Cloverdale Pearl',

'Coachman', 'Corallina', 'Dark Eyes', 'Deutsche Perle', 'Display', 'Dollar Princess', 'Estelle Marie', 'Eva Boerg', 'Fanfare', 'Flash', 'Foncha', 'Fountains Abbey', 'Garden News', 'Gardenmeister Bonstedt', 'Denii', 'Golden Marinka', 'Fraf Witte', 'Hidcote Beauty', 'Jack of Hearts', 'Jack Shahan', 'Joan Goy', 'Joanne', 'John Grooms', 'Joy Patmore', 'Katrina Thompson', 'La Campanella', 'Lady Thumb', 'Lena', 'Leonora', 'Lisa', 'Lord Byron', 'Madame Cornelissen', 'Madeleine Sweeney', 'Marcus Graham', 'Margaret Pilkington', 'Marin Glow', 'Mini Rose', 'Mrs. Marshall', 'Mrs. Popple', 'Natasha Sinton', 'Nellie Nuttall', 'Orange Drops', 'Orange Flare', 'Orange Queen', 'Pacquesa', 'Patio Princess', 'Phyllis', 'Pink Fantasia', 'Rose of Castile', 'Royal Velvet', 'Rufus the Red', 'Ruth', 'Santa Cruz', 'Sealand Prince', 'Sierra Blue', 'Strawberry Sundae', 'Superstar', 'Swingtime', 'Sylvia Barker', 'Tango Queen', 'Thalia', 'Thom Thumb', 'Vivienne Thompson', 'Waltzing Matilda', 'Westminster Chimes', 'White Ann', 'White Pixie', 'White Spider'

Garden Jargon Word Search

H	C	D	N	T	M	F	F	A	E	G	K
H	S	G	L	A	E	O	R	O	V	C	G
A	H	I	O	O	E	N	P	U	A	R	I
R	C	L	L	T	M	U	D	B	T	A	D
D	L	A	I	B	T	F	H	E	D	V	E
S	U	D	C	O	A	C	A	N	R	I	L
C	M	Q	P	Z	N	T	E	E	R	T	B
A	Y	A	K	I	U	M	S	N	L	L	U
P	S	G	P	V	A	A	N	E	T	U	O
E	D	A	E	H	D	A	E	D	I	C	D
A	X	R	B	D	U	U	T	G	H	D	X
H	H	B	E	J	K	X	I	K	C	K	E

Amend   *To improve the soil*
Chit   *To nick or somehow breach a seed coat*
Cultivar   *Cultivated variety*
Deadhead   *To remove a spent flower*
Double-dig   *To tortuously overwork the soil*
Establish   *To root well into the garden*
Foetid   *Stinky*
Hardscape   *The nonplant part of a garden*
Leaf mold   *Decomposed leaves*
Loam   *A soil equally comprised of sand, silt, and clay*
Mulch   *Material spread on the ground to conserve moisture and reduce weeds*
Pinch back   *To remove the growing tip of a stem*

Pot up	*To move a container plant up a size*
Tender	*Not likely to survive the cold*
Turf	*Lawn*

Play Ball!

Outdoor baseball stadiums are famous for the patterns that appear in their turf fields. Groundskeepers worldwide have perfected the art of mowing stripes, logos, and other markings into playing fields through their use of specialized mowing equipment outfitted with bender bars—rollerlike attachments that bend the newly cut grass at a specified angle, which then causes light to reflect off the blades in a certain way. By mowing in different directions intricate patterns of light and dark are created. While difficult to distinguish when standing on the field itself, the angle of TV cameras accentuates the contrast and brings the effect to life.

David Mellor, groundskeeper at Boston's famed Fenway Park, wrote an entire book on the subject titled *Picture Perfect: Mowing Techniques for Lawns, Landscapes, and Sports* (Sleeping Bear Press, 2001).

Crack of the Bat

The Louisville Slugger is the official bat of American Major League Baseball. John Andrew "Bud" Hillerich, son of a German immigrant woodworker and an amateur baseball player, began to turn his own bats and those of his teammates when he joined his father's wood-turning firm as an apprentice in 1880. Stories vary as to how young Bud came to fashion the company's first bat for major league ball players around 1884; however, there is no question that today the Hillerich & Bradsby Company of Louisville, Kentucky, produces about 1 million bats each year for this most American of pastimes. Today's bats are crafted of the highest grade white ash from forests of the northeastern United States with the highest-grade lumber, signified by the number 125, reserved for the professional league; maple, a stronger but heavier wood, accounts for about 30 percent of production.

Take Me Out to the Ballgame

According to Professor Henry T. Wilkinson, a world-renowned expert on the design, building, and maintenance of natural grass sports fields, various strains of Kentucky bluegrass are the best choice for fields in cooler climates, while Bermuda grass is the grass seed of choice for warmer climates. Ryegrass is not generally used except as an overseed mix on winter dormant Bermuda grass, as is it a slippery surface and difficult to repair.

It's in the Rule Book

If a batted ball gets trapped in the ivy-covered outfield wall of Chicago's Wrigley Field, the batter receives a ground rule double.

Rake This

For many, fall leaf cleanup is a pleasant way to spend an autumn afternoon. Not so for those whose gardens contain the raffia palm (*Raphia farinifera*) or the Amazonian bamboo palm (*Raphia taedigera*), both tropical palms whose leaves can achieve lengths of up to 65 feet.

Good Skunk, Bad Skunk

Skunks are generally considered beneficial to the home gardener. They eat armyworms, grasshoppers, tobacco worms, grubs, cutworms, potato beetles, and other garden pests; some states even legislate protection for these members of the weasel family. However, tell that to the individual whose family pet has just been "skunked" for its naive curiosity about these gentle black and white critters, whose only defense when feeling threatened is a malodorous spray fired from anal glands beneath their tails.

It's Official

Many plants have *officianalis* for a species name or other epithet. This indicates that the plant was believed to have healing properties by the individual who named it; early pharmacies or a healer's place of business were originally referred to as an "officinal."

Pine Nuts

The chic garnish of fashionable salads and core ingredient of Italian pesto are the edible seeds of pine trees. While all pines produce edible seeds, only about twenty species have seeds of a size worth harvesting. In North America the seeds of the Colorado pinyon (*Pinus edulis*), single-leaf pinyon (*Pinus monophylla*), and the Mexican pinyon (*Pinus cembroides*) produce the primary harvest. Pine nuts contain about 31 grams of protein per 100 grams of nuts, the highest of any nut or seed. Rich in oils, pine nuts are quick to deteriorate and turn rancid. Once purchased from a reputable, source the seeds should be refrigerated and used in a timely manner.

Summer Pesto

2 cups fresh, tender basil
2 small cloves garlic
¼ cup pine nuts
½ teaspoon sea salt
⅔ cup extra virgin olive oil
½ cup freshly grated Parmesan

Harvest the basil, selecting small leaves over large, as these are less fibrous and more easily broken down. Combine basil, garlic, pine nuts, and sea salt in a food processor and pulse just until coarsely chopped. Slowly add the olive oil with the machine running, and process just until the mixture emulsifies and holds together in a thick sauce. Do not overprocess. Transfer to a bowl, stir in the Parmesan, and serve with well-drained hot pasta, reserving a portion of the pasta cooking water to thin the sauce to a satisfactory consistency. For a fresh take on this summertime favorite, substitute fresh garden mint for a portion of the basil.

Torro Hailstorm Intensity Scale

Intensity	Approximate Size	Description of Damage
H0	Pea	True hail causes little damage
H1	Mothball	Slight damage to plant foliage
H2	Marble	Foliage stripped from trees and plants
H3	Walnut	Glass panes broken, slight damage to car bodies
H4	Golf Ball	Window damage, tree limbs broken, birds killed
H5	Pullet's egg	Large tree limbs broken, small animals injured

Intensity	Approximate Size	Description of Damage
H6	Hen's egg	Damage to roof structures and brick walls
H7	Tennis ball	Roofs shattered, serious risk of injury to all exposed
H8	Softball	Roofs collapse, small trees split, serious injury to all exposed
H9	Grapefruit	Concrete roofs breached, large trees knocked down, fatal injury potential to all exposed
H10	Melon	Brick houses at severe risk, likely fatal injuries to all exposed

Leaf Peeping

Why do leaves change color in the autumn? Plants take up water through their roots and absorb carbon dioxide from the air through pores in their leaves. In the presence of sun the plant is able to convert these two elements into glucose, a form of sugar that the plant uses as an energy source for growing. This process is called photosynthesis ("putting together with light"). Chlorophyll, the green pigment in plants, is the chemical catalyst for this process. In autumn the days shorten until there is not enough daylight present to support continued photosynthesis and chlorophyll disappears from the leaves, revealing the underlying warm colors. With the onset of cool night temperatures, the remaining glucose trapped in the leaves is transformed into the characteristic red, orange, and gold tones of fall. The most brilliant fall color is produced when plants experience regular moisture at the beginning of autumn coupled with cooling temperatures and shortened day length.

The Garden Conservancy

Frank Cabot founded the Garden Conservancy to ensure that exceptional American gardens would survive their gardeners. Since 1989 the following gardens have been preserved and maintained:

Alcatraz Island, San Francisco, CA
The Chase Garden, Orting, WA
The Elizabeth Lawrence Garden, Charlotte, NC
The Fells, the John Hay National Wildlife Refuge, Newbury, NH
Greenwood Gardens, Short Hills, NJ
Hollister House Garden, Washington, CT
The John P. Humes Japanese Stroll Garden, Mill Neck, NY
Montrose, Hillsborough, NC
Peckerwood Garden, Hempstead, TX
Rocky Hills, Mount Kisco, NY
The Ruth Bancroft Garden, Walnut Creek, CA
Van Vleck House and Gardens, Montclair, NJ
Yew Dell Gardens, Crestwood, KY

Bitters

The single-most widely distributed bar item in the world is Angostura bitters, developed in 1824 by Dr. J. Siegert as a tonic to treat fatigue and stomach ailments. It is a secret blend of more than forty tropical herbs, plant extracts, and spices. The mixture is, as the name suggests, of a bitter flavor and is known both as a digestive aid and appetite stimulant. For this reason bitters are often a component of pre- or postmeal cocktails, where they lend flavor and a dry zest.

Champagne Cocktail

Place a sugar cube in the bottom of a substantial champagne flute and soak with a couple of dashes of Angostura bitters. Slowly fill flute with chilled champagne or sparkling wine and garnish with a twist of lemon.

CLEM-A-Tis or Clem-*A*-Tis?

These beautiful, free-flowering, and beloved climbing vines in their many cool colors and various forms are a garden staple throughout the temperate gardening world. Whether they drape a picket fence in Iowa, are carefully trained on pillars in a rose garden, or are let loose to clamber up huge trees on country estates, clematis lend a charming grace note to gardens both cottage and formal.

The question is not whether to grow this "Queen of the Garden" but *how*, given the somewhat arcane pruning rules for the various forms that can stymie even the most learned gardener. While incorrect pruning will not kill a clematis vine, it will greatly affect the flowering for that season.

Clematis are divided into the following three pruning groups, with Group B having two subcategories:

Group A: Varieties flower in the spring on growth produced in the previous growing season. Any pruning should be limited to tidying and cutting out any weak or dead stems after the plant has finished blooming in May or June. Delayed or severe pruning will reduce the number of blooms the following spring. Examples: The popular Montana varieties, the early spring blooming evergreen *Clematis armandii*, as well as *C. alpina* and *C. macropetala*.

Group B: Group B1 includes those varieties that bloom on mature growth from the previous season. A typical bloom pattern would be a heavy flush of bloom May–June, followed by a second smaller bloom flush in the fall on growth produced and matured in the current season. Group B2 includes those varieties that bloom simultaneously on last year's growth and the current season's growth, producing a continuous flush of blooms throughout the summer.

Group B varieties are lightly pruned in late winter or early spring to remove dead or weak wood and evenly space the remaining stems to best show off flowers. If plants in this group have been neglected or have grown into a tangled mess, a severe cutting back of most of the old growth is recommended to renew the vine. Examples: Most of the large-flowered, summer-blooming hybrids.

Group C: Varieties bloom only on the current season's growth, with flowers beginning in summer and continuing through the fall. Plants should be cut back to the strongest 2 buds on each stem roughly 10–12 inches from the ground. Examples: The ever popular large, purple-flowered *C. Jackmanii* as well as the smaller-flowered yet profusely blooming *C. vitacella* varieties.

Root Words

Hoe   *From the Old French houe.*

Prune   *From the Old French proignior, "to round off."*

Orchard   *From the Old English ortgeard, derived from the Latin hortus, meaning garden, and geard meaning yard.*

Seed   *From the Old English saed, which is related to the Dutch zaad, the German saat, and the English sow.*

Shrub   *From the Old English scrubb or scrybb wood to describe more than one. Closely related is the Norwegian skrubbebaer, meaning a dwarf hardwood plant. From these we get the English scrub to define low-growing, rough woody plants.*

Flower   *From the Middle English flour, derived from the Old French flour and flor, which originated from the Latin flos and flor.*

Garden   *From the Middle English gardin, closely related to the Old French of Germanic origin gart.*

Dirt   *A variant of the Middle English drit, meaning filth, excrement, or mud.*

Root   *From the Middle English rot.*

Dandelion *From the Middle English dent-de-lioun and Old French dentdelion, literally "tooth of the lion," referring to the incised leaves of the plant.*

Flower or Garden-Related Cities

Bloom, KS
Bluebell, UT
Cherry, IL
Columbine, CO
Daisy, GA
Daisy, KY
Daisy, MO
Flower, WV
Forest, IN
Garden, MI
Larkspur, CA
Larkspur, CO
Leaf, MS
Lily, KY
Lily, SD
Lily, WI
Magnolia, AL
Magnolia, AR
Magnolia, DE
Magnolia, IA
Magnolia, IL
Magnolia, KY
Magnolia, MN
Magnolia, MS
Magnolia, NC
Magnolia, NJ
Magnolia, OH
Magnolia, TX
Meadow, SD

Meadow, TX
Meadow, UT
Orchid, FL
Petal, MS
Rose, NE
Spring, TX
Strawberry, AZ
Strawberry, CA
Sunflower, MS
Violet, LA
Weed, CA
Weed, NM
Willow, OK
Willow, AK
Willow, NY

First Flower of Spring

Always a highlight of the year, the day on which you discover the first flower of spring indicates the following:

Monday	*Good fortune*
Tuesday	*Success*
Wednesday	*Marriage*
Thursday	*Falling profits*
Friday	*Wealth*
Saturday	*Misfortune*
Sunday	*Impending good luck*

in time of daffodils

in time of daffodils(who know
the goal of living is to grow)
forgetting why, remember how

in time of lilacs who proclaim
the aim of waking is to dream,
remember so(forgetting seem)

in time of roses(who amaze
our now and here with paradise)
forgetting if,remember yes

in time of all sweet things beyond
whatever mind may comprehend,
remember seek(forgetting find)

and in a mystery to be
(when time from time shall set us free)
forgetting me,remember me

—E. E. CUMMINGS (1894–1962), AMERICAN POET

Cinematic Gardens and Gardeners

City Lights (1931): Classic Charlie Chaplin, with the ending scene where the once-blind flower girl says, "Yes, I can see now," as she hands the Little Tramp a flower.

Frankenstein (1931): With the once-deleted but now-restored scene between the monster and the little girl standing beside a lake tossing petals onto its surface. When his petals are gone the monster innocently tosses the little girl in the lake, figuring she would float as well.

Flowers and Trees (1932): Walt Disney's first full-color cartoon.

Wizard of Oz (1939): With the famous scene of characters running through a field of sleep-inducing poppies.

Fantasia (1940): With its "Pastoral" segment.

Alice in Wonderland (1951): Disney's version of the book by Lewis Carroll, featuring talking flowers and the Queen of Hearts's rose garden.

The Little Shop of Horrors (1960): Basis for the Broadway hit musical. A young florist develops a man-eating plant.

My Fair Lady (1964): In which a humble flower girl is transformed into a "real" lady.

Sound of Music (1965): The Von Trapp family performs "Edelweiss," the Austrian national anthem, in defiance of the Nazis and makes their famed escape.

Poppies Are Also Flowers (1966): Little-known movie concerning the heroin trade in the Middle East.

Camelot (1967): Featuring the song, "The Lusty Month of May."

Cold Comfort Farm (1968): In which a city girl visits a farm and plants some flowers with beautiful results.

The Godfather (1972): Don Corleone has a heart attack and dies while spraying the tomatoes in a garden.

Texas Chainsaw Massacre (1974): What happens when a garden implement falls into the wrong hands.

Chinatown (1974): Natural resources versus abusive political power.

Attack of the Killer Tomatoes (1978): A comedic/horror/sci-fi flick with the usual cast of quirky scientists. Followed by the sequel *Return of the Killer Tomatoes* (1988).

Being There (1979): A simple-minded groundskeeper, played by Peter Sellers, becomes known for his modest and inadvertently existential way of looking at life.

Jean de Florrette (1986): A picturesque French village squabbles over water rights crucial to the cultivation of a field of commercial cut flowers.

L'homme qui plantait des arbres (1987): Based on the book of the same name (*The Man Who Planted Trees*), it tells the story of a determined shepherd who personally cultivates a magnificent forest on a formerly desolate site.

Field of Dreams (1989): Cornfields, baseball, and memory. The summer of 1988, when the movie was shot, was one of record drought in the Midwest. Water was brought in to irrigate the cornfield for proper growth, and the thriving field was later plowed under for plot purposes—which was met with bewilderment by real-life area farmers whose own crops were suffering.

Edward Scissorhands (1990): Johnny Depp is the truly bizarre gardener with a gift for topiary and a very tenuous grasp on reality.

The Grasscutter (1990): A member of the Loyalist UVF (Ulster Volunteer Force) goes into hiding as a landscaper in New Zealand, but the Belfast violence catches up to him.

Green Card (1990): A marriage of convenience is a small price to pay to secure a New York apartment with a fabulous greenhouse.

The Hand that Rocks the Cradle (1992): With its drop-dead (literally) gorgeous green house.

Lawn Mower Man (1992): A series of experiments involving mind-altering drugs and virtual reality turn a simple gardener into a roaring genius.

The Secret Garden (1993): A young orphaned English girl is sent to be raised by her uncle. Left to her own devices she discovers a garden and the secrets it holds.

Weedkiller (1995): A garden tool wielding landscaper takes to "weeding" out the human race.

Bed of Roses (1996): Shy florist gets the girl through his gifts of flowers (yawn). Not to be confused with the 1933 film of the same title where two reformed hookers leave prison determined to find a good life with rich men.

Fargo (1996): With its infamous use of a garden chipper to dispose of a body.

A Bug's Life (1998): With one of its several famous lines, "shoo, fly, don't bother me."

Antz (1998): What are the chances of two bug movies in a single year?

Saving Grace (2000): An avid gardener switches from growing flowers to marijuana in a money-making scheme designed to save her home from repossession.

Greenfingers (2000): Features a prison work program in horticulture whose inmate participants are invited to create a garden for the Chelsea Garden Show.

Everything Is Illuminated (2005): With an amazing scene where Elijah Wood strolls up a path bordered on both sides by fields of sunflowers.

"We have descended into the garden and caught three hundred slugs. How I love the mixture of the beautiful and the squalid in gardening. It makes it so lifelike."

—EVELYN UNDERHILL (1875–1941),
ANGLICAN WRITER ON MYSTICISM, NOVELIST,
AND METAPHYSICAL POET

Feed Me!

Carnivorous plants are primarily native to boggy regions with acid soil containing little or no nitrogen. These plants have evolved to derive this necessary nutrient—absent in their natural environment—by "trapping" the bodies of insects, reptiles, and other small mammals. While the actual method of trapping varies with each plant type, once captured prey are first drowned and then digested by liquid secretions.

PPAF (Plant Permit Applied For)

It is becoming ever more common to see the initials PPAF after a plant's botanical name, indicating a plant patent has been applied for. Plant patents, introduced into American law in the 1930s, extend 20 years from the filing of the patent application and grant exclusive propagation rights to the patent holder. Licensed production of the plant generates royalties paid to the patent holder. Trademarks and registrations, on the other hand, are a marketing tool used to establish and reinforce a "brand."

A plant may be patented under one name and trademarked under another; for instance, *Hydrangea macrophylla* 'Bailmer' PPAF also bears the trademarked name Endless Summer Hydrangea. This plant was endlessly promoted in full-page, glossy magazine ads depicting a young woman's beautiful flip-flop-clad feet, toes alluringly painted a pastel blue, poised in front of a gorgeous blooming hydrangea under the headline, "What if Summer Never Ended?" The campaign worked: consumers had to have this first-ever large-flowered hydrangea that would bloom on old and new wood, thus securing their piece of the gardener's dream of a never-ending summer.

How to Grow Big, Blowsy, Buxom Begonias

- *Place tuber, rounded side down, 1-inch deep in a plastic or clay pot. Of critical importance is a well-drained potting mix, as begonias will not tolerate an overly wet or soggy soil.*
- *Provide a filtered light or partial shade exposure. While subject to leaf burn in too much sun, the more light a begonia receives shy of burning, the larger and more numerous the blooms.*
- *Allow the surface of the soil to dry between watering. To increase flower size and extend the blooming period, feed with a liquid fertilizer according to package directions every 2 weeks during the summer in place of a regular watering.*
- *Refrain from placing begonias outdoors until all danger of frost is past and temperatures are steadily warming. At the end of the growing season tubers should be lifted and stored in a frost-free location for the winter.*
- *When placing begonia plants into a container composition or garden bed, see to it that the points of the leaves are facing forward, as most of the flowers will face in this direction.*

Citrus Throughout the Year

While generally available year-round, various citrus peak in terms of flavor and abundance in the following months:

Blood orange .... *February–May*
Orange .... *March–May*
Grapefruit .... *May–September*
Lime............... *August–April*
Navel orange......... *November–January*
Satsuma/mandarin .... *November–March*
Meyer lemon......... *November–January*
Lemon .... *December–September*
Kumquat............ *December–March*

Fern Spore Print Instructions

Denizens of woodlands both temperate and tropical, ferns are vascular plants that do not produce seed; instead they replicate by spore. To capture a lasting image of the elegant form of a fern leaf, select a frond on which fertile spores are apparent on the backside, called a "sporophyll." Place the frond, spore-side down, on a sheet of cream or white paper and leave undisturbed for 6–8 hours. During this time the dustlike spores will disperse, creating an intricately patterned image of the frond. Protect the resulting fern print with an artist's fixative and mount behind glass. At one time fern spores were believed to possess the power of making anyone who held them invisible.

Ten Herbs to Treat Insomnia

California poppy (*Eschscholzia californica*)
Chamomile (*Anthemis nobilis*)
Hops (*Humulus lupulus*)
Kava kava (*Piper methysticum*)
Lavender (*Lavandula officinalis*)
Lemon balm (*Melissa officinalis*)
Passionflower (*Passiflora incarnate*)
Skullcap (*Scutellaria lateriflora*)
Saint-John's-wort (*Hypericum perforatum*)
Valerian (*Valeriana officinalis*)

Ten Herbs to Remain Alert

Black tea (*Camellia sinensis*)
Cayenne pepper (*Capsicum baccatum*)
Fennel seed (*Foeniculum vulgare*)
Ginger (*Zingiber officinale*)
Ginkgo (*Ginkgo biloba*)
Gotu kola (*Centella asiatica*)
Guarana (*Paullinia cupana*)
Peppermint (*Mentha* x *piperita*)
Rosemary (*Rosemarinus officinalis*)
Siberian ginseng (*Eleutherococcus senticosus*)

Bottle Tree

Bottle trees, sometimes called the "poor man's stained glass," are primarily a Southern tradition first brought to the United States by African slaves in the eighteenth century, who placed them in gardens to protect their homes from evil. It was commonly believed that malevolent spirits were attracted to the colorful glass; once trapped inside the bottles, these spirits were then destroyed by the morning sun. To this day on a drive through the South you will come across shiny colored and clear glass bottles threaded onto the branches of a living or dead tree where they catch the light and glitter like jewels in the sun with not an evil spirit in sight.

The Crowning Touch

To create a tire crown planter, you will need:

- *1 old tire, preferably not steel-belted or multi-ply.*
- *Utility knife with a sharp blade.*
- *Brute strength and a warm sunny day. The finished planter will entail turning the tire completely inside out, a task more easily accomplished with a warm tire. If the weather is not cooperating, bring the tire indoors the night before to warm it up.*

Wash the tire thoroughly with a stiff brush and household cleaner to remove grease and road grime. Lay the tire on its side and with the utility knife begin to cut several inches outside the tire's tread. Working in a circular direction, continue to cut around the diameter of the tire until you can remove an O-shaped ring from the middle of the tire.

Turn the tire on to its other side to begin the "crown" cut. Beginning just inside the edge of the tread, slice an angled cut nearly to the center hole and back. Continue in this zigzag manner completely around the tire. The piece you will remove this time will be star-shaped.

Turn the tire inside out by grasping a point of the "crown" and pulling it through the center hole. Continue point by point around the tire to fully invert it, creating the classic planter shape.

In warm regions it is customary to paint the finished tire planter for decorative appeal as well as to reflect the heat of the midday sun.

Houseleeks as Homeowner's Insurance

Houseleeks (*Sempervivum sempervirens*), a tough succulent able to grow in shallow soil and exposed locations, were once planted on rooftops where it was believed they would fend off fire, hunger, plague, lightning, bad luck, and war.

Garden Superstitions

- *Homes were decked with holly and mistletoe berries to ward off evil spirits, a pagan belief now firmly a part of the Christian holiday season ritual.*
- *A braid of garlic keeps vampires away.*
- *Carry an acorn in your pocket to bring about good luck.*
- *Ivy growing on a house protects its inhabitants from witchcraft and evil.*
- *If you catch a falling leaf on the first day of autumn you will not catch a cold in the coming winter.*
- *Plant rosemary by the doorstep to keep witches away.*
- *Four-leaf clovers not only bring good luck, they also offer protection from magic spells and jesting fairies.*
- *To dream of a vegetable garden indicates increased prosperity with hard work and patience.*
- *To dream of a flower garden foretells peace, love, and comfort.*
- *To dream of a weedy garden signals neglect of spiritual needs.*

Another Weather Portent

A rainbow in the eastern sky,
The morrow will be fine and dry.
A rainbow in the west that gleams,
Rain tomorrow falls in streams.

Passionflower as Allegory

The passionflower (*Passiflora incarnata*), a vigorous twining vine native to the Americas, was given its name by Jesuit missionaries who interpreted its curious bloom as a metaphor for the passion of Christ:

5 petals and 5 sepals	*Represent the ten apostles present at the crucifixion of Jesus*
5 stamens	*Represent the five wounds inflicted on Jesus as he hung on the cross*
3 styles	*Represent the nails in the cross*
Circle of hairlike rays	*Represent the crown placed on the head of the "king of the Jews"*

When native Indians were seen eating the fruit of this vine, the missionaries took it as a sign of their "hunger" for redemption.

The One That Got Away . . .

These seemingly good garden ideas have gone horribly wrong:

- *English ivy (Hedera helix):* An aggressive, invasive, introduced species once valued in landscaping for its ability to thrive in shade with little care and to produce rapid growth to form a dense evergreen groundcover able to suppress any other plant growth. Ironically it is these same characteristics that pose such a threat to green belts and native forests when ivy escapes the confines of cultivation.

- *European starling (Sturnus vulgaris):* While clearly not a plant, the starling is certainly a common resident—some might even say pest—found in gardens, parks, and green areas throughout the United States. A literary society intent on introducing into America all the birds mentioned in the writings of Shakespeare released the birds in New York's Central Park in the 1890s. Easily adapting to man-made environments, their population is estimated to have grown from those original 100 birds to in excess of 200 million. These highly social birds flock in great numbers and form communal roosts at night. Their numbers are greatest during fall and winter, when flocks of thousands blacken the sky and harass other birds, people, and animals alike.

- *Himalayan blackberry (Rubus discolor):* Native to western Europe and introduced to the United States in the late nineteenth century as a cultivated crop grown for its delicious but seedy berries. Supple stems, or canes, sucker profusely, rooting to form new plants wherever they touch the ground and quickly forming an impenetrable thorny thicket tremendously difficult to eradicate and capable of smothering everything in its path. If the thorns, canes, and vigor were not enough, seed is readily dispersed by the many birds and animals that feed on the berries.

❦ *Kudzu (Pueraria lobata):* Planted during the Great Depression by the Soil Conservation Service in an effort to preserve agricultural fields and assist in erosion control. It is estimated that more than 7 million acres of the South have been swallowed by this vigorous vine.

❦ *Old-man's-beard (Clematis vitalba):* At once a sentimental favorite for its sweet-smelling, late-summer bloom and a menacing threat to everything in its path. Stems that trail along the ground have the ability to root at every node. With up to 30 feet of new growth each year, in addition to the production of thousands of seeds spread by wind and water, this vine can quickly overtake the garden, escaping to roadsides, greenbelts, and any area of disturbed land. This clambering vine is capable of smothering huge trees, blocking the light trees need to thrive, and even bringing down large branches with its weight.

❦ *Scouring rush (Equisetum hyamale):* Not so much introduced as frighteningly indomitable, this is a primitive plant akin to ferns that has been around since dinosaurs roamed the Earth. Woe be to the naive gardener who plants it in the garden as a dark green, vertical accent. Happiest in damp soil, scouring rush will spread like the wind, insinuating itself permanently into every nook and cranny, and is immune to even the strongest herbicide.

🌺 *Touch-me-not (Impatiens balsamina):* More of an annoyance than an actual threat, this shade-loving, summer-blooming annual is seldom found in the nursery trade but is generally passed from one gardener to the next, a clue as to the vigor of its progeny that produce seed from one year to the next. The common name "touch-me-not" is derived from the coiled seed pods' ability to hurl seed far and wide at the merest touch. With blooms that appear in pink, purple, red, coral, orange, and white on plants that can get to 3 feet tall, there is little doubt as to this plant's beauty, but proceed with caution.

"Hurrah! . . . it is a frost!—the dahlias are dead."

—R. S. SURTEES (1805–64), ENGLISH SOLICITOR AND WRITER

That Which We Call a Rose

rose	*English*
nam toe	*Dutch*
s'est levé	*French*
stieg	*German*
αυξήθηκε	*Greek*
è aumentato	*Italian*
levantou-se	*Portuguese*
поднял	*Russian*
subió	*Spanish*

Water Wisdom

- *Water is constant. The same amount of water is present on our planet today as when the Earth was formed millions of years ago, and continually cycle through a system of evaporation, condensation, precipitation, and infiltration.*

- *Water is the only substance on Earth naturally occurring in three forms—liquid, gas, and solid.*

- *The Earth's surface is 75 percent covered in water. Of that, 97 percent is found in oceans and 2 percent is locked up in ice caps and glaciers. The remaining 1 percent is potable water.*

- *An average household in this country consumes 107,000 gallons of water a year. Of that, an estimated 30 percent is used for outdoor purposes—gardening, car washing, pools, and ponds.*

- *An outdoor spigot can pump 5–10 gallons of water per minute (think of that the next time the sprinkler is inadvertently left on).*

- *An inch of rainfall drops 7,000 gallons, nearly 30 tons, on a 60- by 180-foot piece of land, about the size of an average suburban household property.*

- *A birch tree transpires (gives off) approximately 70 gallons of water a day.*

- *A tomato is 95 percent water.*

- *Humans are 60 percent water; elephants are 70 percent water.*

Necessary Garden Tools

Spade: Flat-blade, square-tipped shovel with a long handle used for digging and turning soil.

Shovel: Scooped blade with a pointed tip for cutting into established plantings and turf. A short-handled version with a narrow blade, called a "poaching shovel," facilitates digging in crowded beds with the least disturbance of neighboring plants.

Garden fork: A short-handled model with squared tines is valuable for turning soil and mixing in garden amendments.

Pruning shears: Those with a sharp, bypass blade that can be sharpened and comfortable handles will greatly reduce effort. You get what you pay for.

Hand trowel: For digging close at hand. Choose a comfortable handle and a sturdy forged blade with an offset integral shaft to provide leverage. Avoid cheap trowels prone to bend at the tip with the first gardening session.

Pruning saw: Choose a folding model with a narrow blade for working in close quarters among trees and shrubs and a sturdy blade that will not bend, with a good locking mechanism that latches securely for safety's sake.

Hoe: This old-fashioned garden staple has fallen into disuse. With its long handle and sharp blade, a hoe is valuable for scuffling away young weeds and unwanted seedlings from a comfortable standing position, saving an aging gardener's back.

Rake: Flexible, lightweight tines and a long handle greatly facilitate garden cleanup chores.

How to Dry Flowers

While you might employ a microwave oven or a silica sand substance, what follows is perhaps the easiest way to dry flowers:

1. Select flowers and harvest after the morning dew has dried.
2. Shorten the stem to the desired length, removing any foliage or damaged parts.
3. Gather flower stems in small bunches and secure with a rubber band or other tie. (A rubber band will accommodate shrinkage in the flower stems as they dry while still holding the bunch together.) For larger blooms such as peonies, roses, or hydrangeas, hang flowers to dry individually.
4. Hang flower bunches or single stems upside down in a well-ventilated, dark, and dry room. Blooms will be dried and ready for use in 4–7 days.
5. Store dried flowers out of direct sun to preserve color.

Suggested Blooms for Drying

Baby's breath (*Gypsophila paniculata*)
Bachelor's button (*Centaurea cyanus*)
Bells of Ireland (*Molucella laevis*)
Bishop's-weed (*Ammi majus*)
Blue sage (*Salvia farinacea*)
Cockscomb (*Celosia*)

Cornflower (*Centaurea cyanus*)
Edelweiss (*Leontopodium alpinum*)
Everlasting (*Helichrysum petiolatum*)
Feverfew (*Chrysanthemum parthenium*)
Fountain grass (*Pennisetum*)
Globe amaranth (*Gomphrena globosa*)
Globe thistle (*Echinops ritro*)
Honesty (*Lunaria annua*)
Immortelle (*Xeranthemum annuum*)
Larkspur (*Colsolida ambigua*)
Lavender (*Lavandula*)
Love-in-a-mist seed heads (*Nigella damascena*)
Love-lies-bleeding (*Amaranthus*)
Ornamental oregano (*Origanum laevigatum*)
Pampas grass (*Cortaderia selloana*)
Poppy seed heads (*Papaver somniferum*)
Quaking grass (*Briza maxima*)
Roses (*Rosa*)
Safflower (*Carthamus tinctorius*)
Scarlet sage (*Salvia*)
Sea lavender (*Limonium latifolium*)
Squirreltail grass (*Hordeum jubatum*)
Statice (*Goniolimon tartaricum*)
Strawflower (*Helichrysum bracteatum*)
Sunflower (*Helianthus*)
Sweet Annie (*Artemesia annua*)
Teasel (*Dipsacus fullonum*)
Yarrow (*Achillea millefolium*)

Fried Green Tomatoes

When cool weather arrives before all the tomatoes have ripened, savvy garden cooks relish this seasonal treat.

Unripe (green) tomatoes big enough for slicing
1–2 eggs
Cornmeal
Salt, pepper, and cayenne
Bacon grease or other oil for frying
Sour cream (optional)

Slice tomatoes ½-inch thick and drain on paper towels. Crack the egg(s) into a shallow soup bowl and lightly beat with a fork. Place cornmeal in another shallow soup bowl and season with salt, pepper, and cayenne. Heat the bacon grease or oil in a heavy skillet on the stovetop until hot but not smoking. Working quickly to avoid a soggy end result, first dip tomato slices in egg, turning to coat thoroughly; then dredge in seasoned cornmeal and transfer slices to the skillet. Fry tomatoes over medium heat for about 2–3 minutes per side to brown nicely. Serve at once with a dollop of sour cream.

Horticultural Hall of Fame

Andre Le Notre (1613–1700): Designed the spectacular formal gardens of Versailles.

Capability Brown (1715–83): Popularized pastoral landscapes in reaction to overly formalized gardens.

Andrew Jackson Downing (1815–52): Designed the White House grounds.

Fredrick Law Olmsted (1822–1903): Father of American landscape architecture.

William Robinson (1838–1935): Promoted the use of native plant species mixed with hardy exotic imported species in garden design.

Gertrude Jekyll (1843–1932): Famed English garden designer and colorist.

Jen Jensen (1860–1951): Strong promoter of regional garden style; accredited with developing Midwestern Prairie style.

Beatrix Farrand (1872–1959): First female member of the American Society of Landscape Architects, known for her work in the Arts and Crafts style.

Vita Sackville-West (1892–1962): English author famed for the garden she built at Sissinghurst Castle with her husband Harold Nicholson.

Thomas Church (1902–78): Pioneered the California style of gardens as outdoor living spaces.

Russell Page (1906–85): English landscape architect who designed the justly famed grounds of the PepsiCo world headquarters in New York.

Rosemary Verey (1919–2001): English garden designer best known for her ornamental vegetable garden designs as well as her esteemed client list, which included HRH Prince Charles and Sir Elton John, a fact she never hesitated to mention.

Christopher Lloyd (1921–2006): Beloved, irascible English gardener and writer who championed bold color and mixed plantings requiring less maintenance than the more traditional completely herbaceous perennial border.

Penelope Hobhouse (1929–): Esteemed garden writer, garden historian, and garden designer with projects throughout the world.

Plants Mentioned in the Bible

Plants of utility and sustenance: Acacia, almond, aloe, apple, balm of Gilead, barley, bean, bramble, broom, calamus, cane, caper, cinnamon, cattail, cedar, coriander, cotton, cumin, cypress, dill, fig, flax, galbanum, gall, garlic, gourd, grape, henna, hyssop, laurel, leeks, lentil, lily of the valley, mandrake, melon, millet, mint, mustard, myrtle, nettles, oak, olive, onion, palm, papyrus, pine, pistachio, plane tree, pomegranate, poplar, reed, rose of Sharon, rue, rush, saffron, sorghum, styrax, tamarisk, thistle, tumbleweed, walnut, willow, wormwood.

Ripe for Botanical Blunders

Argemone, Callirrhoë, Eschscholtzia, Glaucium, Macleaya, Meconopsis, Papaver, Romneya, Stylophorum: All plants whose common name is "poppy."

Ajania, Arctanthemum, Coleostephus, Glebionis, Leucanthemum, Nipponanthemum, Tanacetum, Pyrethropsis, Pyrethrum: All plants whose common name is "chrysanthemum."

"We do not all want to float endlessly among silvers, grays, and tender pinks in the gentle nicotiana-laden ambient of a summer's gloaming. Some prefer a bright, brash midday glare with plenty of stuffing."

—CHRISTOPHER LLOYD (1921–2006),
GARDEN MAVERICK AND COLORIST

Deer-Resistant Plants

While no plant is safe from browsing if the animal is so moved, the following have been found to be the most resistant to deer damage:

Trees and shrubs: Ash, barberry, bottlebrush, boxwood, broom, burning bush, butterfly bush, California and Pennsylvania bayberry, California bay, California lilac, cotoneaster, daphne, Douglas fir, eastern red cedar, eucalyptus, flowering currant, germander, heath, heavenly bamboo, holly, juniper, kerria, kinnikinnick, madrone, Mexican orange, some oaks, Oregon grape, ornamental sage, palm, pomegranate, red maple, rhododendron (not azaleas), rock rose, rosemary, salal, silverberry, smoke tree, South African honeybush, spruce, Saint-John's-wort, stone pine, strawberry tree, yew.

Perennials, vines, and bulbs: Artichoke, asparagus, bamboo, bear's-breeches, bee balm, begonia, bird-of-paradise, bishop's-cap, black-eyed Susan, bleeding heart, buckwheat, California poppy, calla lily, catmint, chives, cyclamen, daffodil, daisy, dead nettle, dusty miller, ferns, foxglove, hosta, iris, Japanese anemone, jasmine, Kenilworth ivy, lamb's ears, lavender, lenten rose, lily of the Nile, lupine, monkshood, New Zealand flax, Oriental poppy, most ornamental grasses, red-hot poker, snowflakes, spurge, star jasmine, sweet woodruff, tulip, wake-robin, wormwood, yarrow.

Rat Patrol

The common brown rat (*Rattus norvegicus*, also called the Norwegian or sewer rat) is a destructive pest capable of inflicting a great deal of destruction on newly planted bulbs, emerging perennials, and vegetable gardens as well as damaging gardens and structures with their burrowing, gnawing, feeding, and subsequent contamination.

To protect the garden against ravaging rodents:

- 🐀 *Maintain sewage and drainage pipes in good repair.*
- 🐀 *When feeding birds, use a platform feeder or a hanging net and be sure to clean up any seed that falls on the ground.*
- 🐀 *Refrain from feeding wildlife in the garden.*
- 🐀 *Ensure that dog and cat food is not left unattended, and remove the bowl for cleaning as soon as it is empty.*

- *Position all pet cages at least 8 inches above the ground, placing them on a solid surface to make cleaning any food spillage beneath them easier.*
- *Do not put meat or other nonvegetable/fruit food waste onto compost piles.*
- *Outbuildings and sheds should be sealed so that rats cannot gain access; pay particular attention to gaps around door and window openings.*
- *Do not store bags of grain, plant-based fertilizer, or seed stock in unsecured outdoor buildings.*
- *Maintain good garden hygiene, removing any spoiled fruit or vegetable matter immediately, and do not allow debris to pile up, which might make for a good nesting site.*

Hummingbirds

One of the most beloved birds, the hummingbird is romanticized and fawned over by gardeners and nongardeners alike. In fact these birds are greedy, highly competitive, power mongering, territorial fascists keenly intent on identifying a territory and protecting it from all incursions, human or otherwise, at any cost.

Plants to attract hummingbirds: Beardtongue, bee balm, butterfly bush, catmint, clove pink, columbine, coral bells, cypress vine, daylily, desert candle, flag iris, flowering tobacco, foxglove, fuchsia, hollyhock, honeysuckle vine, larkspur, lily, lobelia, lupine, monkey flower, petunia, pincushion flower, red-hot poker, scarlet runner bean, scarlet sage, soapwort, summer phlox, trumpet creeper vine, verbena, weigela. (*Note:* Whenever possible select varieties whose blooms appear in shades of red and orange.)

The Molecular Structure of Chlorophyll

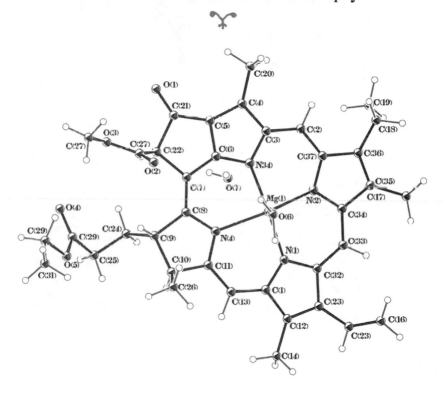

DIAGRAM COURTESY OF WWW.RECIPROCALNET.ORG

Index

National Register of Big Trees, 81
natural air conditioners, 171
nighttime scented plants, 41
noxious weeds, 194
nutrients, primary, secondary, and
micro-, 51–52

O

officianalis, 208
O'Keefe, Georgia, 201
oldest living thing on earth, 150
oldest living tree, 149

P

parsley, 89
passionflower, 229
patron saints of the garden, 130
perennial, 77, 111
permaculture, 181
petal plucking rhyme, 4
pine nuts, 208
plant collectors, deaths of, 113
planting, questions to consider
before, 39
planting rhyme, 92
plants "discovered" by Lewis and
Clark, 134
plants in space, 88
plants mentioned in the Bible, 239
plants mentioned in the writings of
Colette, 170
plants mentioned in the writings of
Shakespeare, 94
pogonip, 13
pots, how to moss, 9
PPAF (plant patent applied for), 222

Q–R

quarantined plants, 140
quincunx, 89
rat patrol, 241
rattan, 129
relief from tension headaches and
stress, 62
root words, 214
rose, the emblem of Venus, 183
Rose Bowl parade stats, 129
rose emoticon, how to make, 89
rose vinegar, 10
roses, old, 125
Run for the Roses, 80

S

safe ice thickness, 13
say it with flowers, 11
scented geraniums, 8
Scofield heat units, 83
seeds, viability of, 4
self-seeding perennials, 33
sexual propagation, 67
shade, degrees of, 124
Sissinghurst's white garden, 85
skunks, 207
slug-be-gone vanishing spray, 50
smell, 62, 65
smudging, 22
snowdrops, 1
splinters and thorns, 185
state flowers, birds, and trees, 60
stone scaping, 90
strawberry varieties, 187
Surtees, R. S., 232
sweet peas, 6

T

temperature conversions, 16
tobacco mosaic virus, 84
tomato varieties, 103–10
tonic tea, 49
Torro Hailstorm Intensity Scale, 209
toxic garden plants, 56
true rosary beads, 9
tuber, 174
turf blends, 46
types of tomatoes, 103

U

Underhill, Evelyn, 221
United States Department of
    Agriculture (USDA), 70
urban agriculture, 182
USDA organic, 131
USDA plant hardiness zones, 42

V

vegetables suitable for container
    gardening, 38
Venus fly trap, 46
Versailles, 142
violet, how to candy, 186
vines, 190

W

water, 233
weather portents, 23, 229
weeds, 34–35, 194
White House National Christmas
    Trees, 100
wicker, 129
wind speed, 14
windchill factor, 102
wood, weight of, 83
world's largest cabbage, 37
world's smallest park, 82
Wrigley Field, 207

X

xeriscape gardening, 24

About the Authors

Lorene Edwards Forkner is a Seattle-based garden designer, writer, and speaker, as well as the owner of Fremont Gardens (www.fremontgardens.com), a regionally well-known specialty nursery. She spent two years on the Perennials and Bulbs selection committee of Great Plant Picks, a plant awards program designed to help home gardeners identify unbeatable plants for their Pacific Northwest gardens. A two-time gold medal winner at the Northwest Flower & Garden Show and recipient of the Founders Cup for her design work in 2003, Lorene seeks to infuse color, texture, and form as well as year-round interest in every garden she creates. In addition to her position on the board of the Northwest Horticultural Society, she is currently one of the NHS representatives on the Pacific Horticulture board. Lorene gardens at home in West Seattle and fully admits she is a garden geek.

Linda Plato was a garden designer whose work was featured on HGTV and at the Northwest Flower & Garden Show. She also wrote about gardening for *Seattle Homes & Lifestyle* and *Pacific Horticulture,* among other publications. She was fascinated with reference works from childhood on and spent a number of years at Microsoft as an editor and program manager converting print reference works into digital formats. Linda Plato succumbed to metastatic breast cancer in 2005.